The Janata Interludes: Democracy, Plurality and Social Change in India

The Janata Interludes: Democracy, Plurality and Social Change in India

Dr. Pavithran K. S.

Vij Books India Pvt Ltd

New Delhi (India)

Published by

Vij Books India Pvt Ltd
(Publishers, Distributors & Importers)
2/19, Ansari Road
Delhi – 110 002
Phones: 91-11-43596460, 91-11-47340674
Mobile: 98110 94883
e-mail: contact@vijpublishing.com
www.vijbooks.com

ISBN: 978-93-89620-17-7 (HB)
ISBN: 978-93-89620-18-4 (ebook)

Dedicated to the memory

of

Prof. K. Vikramadithyan

Contents

Acknowledgements

Over the years I did research on the topic of this book and my teachers and friends have provided invaluable encouragement and assistance. I would like to keep in memory the inspiration given by late Dr. R. Ramakrishnan Nair, formerly Professor and Head of the Department of Politics, University of Kerala to take up 'post-emergency politics' as an apt topic for analysis.

I would also like to thank in particular Dr. N.K. Bhaskaran, Professor and Former Head of the Department of Politics, University of Kerala for his enlightening suggestions through out the completion of this work.

Thanks are also to Dr. C. N. Somarajn, Shri. A.M. Roshan and Dr. V. Rajendran Nair who helped me through inspiring discussions and fruitful comments on the draft, and to Srilatha who offered routine forms of support and assisted him with great patience.

Lastly I am obliged to Vij Books, New Delhi for undertaking the publication of the book.

- Pavithran K.S.

1

Introduction

Every nation arrives at a crossroad, when the existing regime become oppressive and people start looking for an alternative. At this juncture they abandon the uneasy security of a longstanding governing system and opt for the risky experiment of a new political combination. This, the Indian people did in 1977 and again in 1989. These two political experiments were eventful periods in the history of Indian democracy. An evaluative and comparative analysis of these 'Janata' experiments is of great interest to the students of democracy and Indian politics throughout the world.

The largest democracy in the world, which combined miserable poverty and a developing economy, was suspected by many to be an infertile soil for the seeds of democracy. However, the Indian political system succeeded in coping with the pressures and pulls under the statesmanship and charisma of Jawaharlal Nehru with the moral support of the Gandhian and Nationalistic legacy. But by 1975 the compulsions of social forces and the state of the economy prompted Indira Gandhi to declare a state of Emergency, which the Indian people felt oppressive and threatening. Many of her critics alleged that Mrs. Gandhi had resorted to such drastic measures with the objective of sustaining her "dynastic dictatorship". The backlash of this regime and the politics after the historic Lok Sabha elections of March 1977, are of utmost importance to historians and students of Indian politics as well as progressive minded people. The subsequent journey of the new experiment from *total revolution* to total disintegration proved indeed, that Indian faction politics is in general, a question not of principles, but of persons.[1]

The political scene of the later half of 1979 appeared as a barn house after the storm. The all-pervading fragmentation which split and re-split the political parties and never gave way to political reorientation and re-alignment is a perplexing kaleidoscope to observe in retrospect. Out of such choas evolved the Left Front,[2] a political entity with fluctuating fortunes in the future of the country. The Emergency experience proved to be a moment of truth for many in the Left and has led to the realisation that a democratic revolution was a necessary precondition for a true people's revolution. However, the general contour lines of these developments could be discerned in the light of the political upheavals and turbulence of the following decades. The solutions could be found deeper down the crevices of the Indian body politic, factious cliques and is left to the caprices of posterity.

The November 1989 Lok Sabha elections and the formation of the minority National Front Government with the support from outside by the two polar opposites[3] the Bharatiya Janata Party and the Left Front are novel experiments in the Indian political scenario. The collapse of the V.P. Singh government in its fight against casteism and communalism, along with the Left and other progressive elements, visibly headed towards political polarisation and re-alignment of all secular and democratic forces in the country.

The study of a changing political system and new political experiments is always an absorbing vocation to students of political science. Instead of dwelling on the political actions of the past, it is more relevant to apply the standards of evaluation they have developed to contemporary problems. When I started my post graduate studies in 1979, the Janata experiment was at its peak. The first sensations of Janata upheaval was before this and the emergence of disillusionment was slowly visible in the horizon. Closely following these events to the present-day political developments, it is natural for me to take it as an interesting topic for analysis and hence this study.

The general outline of the study is divided into nine chapters. The first is the general introduction, following by seven chapters dealing with particular studies of situations and tendencies of importance. Thus, the chapter on "Back-lash of Emergency" deals with the pre-emergency situation and postulates that there existed, a definite political tendency which may be termed as a 'break-down' of democracy. The origins of such a tendency are sought in the then prevailing socio-economic structures and the whole study is conducted within a historical frame of reference. The study extends to the formation of the Janata Party as a viable alternative.

Unlike the other chapters the third chapter is relatively autonomous and consists mainly of information on the March 1977 elections to the Parliament. The impact of the election on the Indian Political System is also discussed. The fourth chapter is the direct extension of the third and treats post-poll political processes with a special reference to the formation of the Janata Government and developments within the Congress Party.

The fifth chapter is on the promises and performance of the Janata government. It also deals with the failure and disintegration of Janata experiment which may bear the tone of an indictment. The following two chapters are provided with the political developments in India - the 1989 Lok Sabha elections, the formation of the new coalition and the National Front[4] government and the collapse of it due to the inner contradictions of its support-base and the signs of political modernization and development are critically and analytically examined.

The eighth chapter is an analysis of the Indian socio-historic structure with the specific aim of determining why and how it has not been conducive to the emergence of a strong Left-oriented political party. It also treats the efforts made towards the formation of a Left Front comprising the various communist, socialist and other anti-communal and anti-authoritarian forces. The conclusion, is devoted to surmises and conclusions warranted by the foregoing study. It deals with the possibilities of subjecting the facts presented in the earlier chapters to a political analysis and a drawing of logically permissible conclusions.

Notes and References:

1. David Selbourne, *Through the Indian Looking-glass,* Bombay, 1982, p.116.

2. The Left Front consists of the Communist Party of India (Marxist), the Communist Party of India, the Revolutionary Socialist Party and the All-India Forward Bloc.

3. W.H.Morris Jones predicted in early seventies that the most striking confrontation in Indian political thinking is likely to be that between Marxism and Hindu nationalism". See his *The Government of Politics of India,* New Delhi, 1974, p. 258.

4. The National Front was a combination of centrist and regional political parties which includes, Janata Dal, Congress (S), Telugu Desam Party, Dravida Munnetta Kazhagam and Assam Gana Parishad.

2

Back-Lash of Emergency and The Formation of Janata Party

The National Emergency of 1975- 1997 was the first major trial of strength and resilience of India's democracy. The oppressive Emergency laws of this period brought the best out of the divided opposition, and galvanised them into a united force, under Jayaprakash Narayan. By precipitating the seething discontent of the masses, reeling under the oppression of 'dynastic dictatorship', the retaliatory storm gathered and manifested itself in the 1977 election. The election swept away the Emergency regime and put the nascent Janata party on to the throne of power. The election, which was the turning point of post independent India, was hailed as the 'second liberation'[1] of the Indian nation and was named as the new independence of a dormant nation with a submissive will. Thus, the Congress party which had monolithic structure and monopoly of power since independence was replaced by the Janata party, a conglomeration of heterogeneous elements - assuming consensual national status, and which gradually emerged as the embodiment of the nation's hopes and aspirations. For an understanding of these events, we have to discern the roots of the social compulsions and authoritarian tendencies which paved the way for the enigmatic Emergency declaration of June 1975.

The Antecedents of Emergency

June 25th 1975 was free India's darkest hour.[2] Not only was democracy eclipsed, but the whole nation was placed under a pall of fear. In the opinion of Prof. Rajni Kothari, the emergency was the culmination of a process which had begun earlier. As he wrote, "when populist rhetoric is not backed by concrete measures and leads to further aggravation of mass unrest, the only recourse left is to use the coercive power of the state and an increasing use of techniques of repression and terror. The resulting 'authoritarianism' as a political style and a form of management of power, which incidentally emerged long before the Emergency and found its full expression in it, was an answer to two basic factors; the inability of the regime to strike social roots, and its incapacity to perform on the economic front".[3] This basic roots of popular discontent was highlighted by the emergence of Jaya Prakash Narayan in to active politics as spearhead of a new crusading movement.

The first expressions of discontent with Indira Gandhi's regime came when an inner crisis of Congress party was going on due to the abridgement of inner party democracy within the Congress and the imposition of relatively unrepresentative Chief Ministers in the States etc. Norms and rules governing the conduct of public affairs were non-chalantly disregarded, Judges superseded, civil servants asked to become committed and the Press required to fall in line. To top it all, party circles were humming with stories of gross irregularities by the Prime Minister's son- Sanjay Gandhi-with her connivance.[4]

The popular discontent expressed itself initially in spontaneous and sporadic agitations in Gujarat (*Nav Nirman Andolan*) and then in Bihar (*Total Revolution*). In both states the agitations soon acquired the form of a more organised and sustained protest movements. Economic issues like price rise which figured initially as central to the protest, receded early into the background. Instead, as the movements developed, attention turned to electoral malpractices, rampant corruption, and the buying of supporters, within the legislature and the party organs, by those seeking positions of power in the government and in the party. The specific demands of these movements, therefore, were overwhelmingly political in character[5] with the call for the resignation of the Chief Ministers and the dissolution of the State assemblies of both Gujarat and Bihar. These movements were an expression of the fact that substantial sections of the people had over the years, moved from being mere subjects to being aware and concerned citizens no longer willing to sit back and watch politicians play ducks and drakes with the system.

In Gujarat the movement was launched by students in January 1974, which led ultimately to the resignation of the Congress government headed by Chimanbhai Patel. In the light of what happened in Gujarat, Jayaprakash Narayan called for the dissolution of the Bihar legislature. Then there started an agitation with a new move, with the significant part played by the Jana Sangh leadership. The high water-mark of JP's new movement was reached on 6th March, 1975 when he led a mass rally in New Delhi, the like of which had not been witnessed in the capital at any time before, to present a charter of demands to parliament. Then it became clear that there was all chances of a confrontation between the opposition headed by Jayaprakash Narayan and the government headed by Indira Gandhi. To avoid this confrontation and to protect the democratic set up of India, the Congress leaders like Chandrasekhar and Mohan Dharia came forward to bring about a reconciliation between Jayaprakash and Prime Minister Indira Gandhi. But unfortunately, Mrs. Gandhi reacted sharply and asked for the resignation of Mohan Dharia, who was Minister of State for Housing in her cabinet.

When this miscalculated occurrence took place in the governmental level, Morarji Desai launched an indefinite fast on a demand for the ending of presidential rule in Gujarat and the holding of elections to the State assembly. Indira Gandhi was obliged to concede the demand much against her will. Meanwhile the arguments in Raj Narain's election petition against Indira Gandhi had concluded at the Allahabad High Court. By an ironical co-incidence the results in the Gujarat elections and the judgement of Justice J.M.L. Sinha were out in the same week and both came as stunning shocks to Indira Gandhi. In Gujarat elections the Janata Morcha, the opposition coalition won a majority. The greater shock was Justice Sinha's judgement, setting aside her election and debarring her from contesting for parliament for six years. Later on Justice Sinha revealed that D.S. Mathur, who had retired as the Chief Justice of Allahabad High Court had told him a few days before he delivered the judgement that he would be elevated to the Supreme Court if he decided the case in favour of Indira Gandhi.[6] This is one of the best examples to Indira Gandhi's style of functioning during her regime.

Matters came to a head again when on 24th June, Justice V.R. Krishna Iyer, vacation Judge of the Supreme Court, disposed of Indira Gandhi's appeal for extending unconditional stay granted by Justice Sinha, till her appeal before the Supreme Court against the judgement was disposed of and passed orders granting only conditional stay.[7] While Indira Gandhi was considering how to meet the new situation created by Justice Krishna Iyer's judgement the opposition parties led by Jayaprakash Narayan, Charan Singh, Morarji Desai and others held a rally on the Ram Lila grounds in New Delhi at which the opposition announced that they would launch a nationwide agitation to secure the resignation of the Prime Minister Indira Gandhi.[8] At this meeting at which Jayaprakash Narayan repeated his appeal to the police and the military not to carry out unlawful orders from any authority.

Indira Gandhi saw that the danger was from three sides, from the side of the opposition parties from the side of her rivals in her own party and and finally from the side of Judiciary.[9] The problem then was one of survival and not of containment of opposition. She reacted to this 'tripple dangers very much with the support of Congress leaders at different levels all over the country. Taking confidence of her son, Sanjay Gandhi and her other confidents like, Bansilal, S.S.Ray, R.K. Dhawan and V.C. Shukla, on the night of the 25th June, Indian President Fakruddin Ali Ahmed was requested to promulgate the Emergency under article 352 of the Constitution of India, to counter the threat of internal distrubances.

Emergency a Breakdown in Democratic Norms

Simultaneously with the proclamation of Emergency on 25th June 1975, in a round up, all prominent leaders of the non-CPI opposition in the capital and all over the country were arrested and detained under Maintenance of Internal Security Act (MISA). A complete censorship was imposed under Rule 48 of the Defence and Internal Security of India Act, 1971. Following this President issued another order suspending the citizens rights to move the courts under Articles 14, 21 and 22 of the Indian Constitution. This was followed by a ban on twenty-six organizations[10] which came into being by four separate order under rule 33 (1) of the Defence of India Rules, 1971. Thus, the road to 'dictatorship' was made clear and a number of constitutional amendments took place.

The 38th amendment was passed which empowered the President to proclaim any number of Emergencies simultaneously. It also barred the courts from hearing petitions challenging the proclamation of any Emergency or any rules imposed under an Emergency proclamation. Another amendment to the Representation of People's Act 1951, intended retrospectively to legalise the practices which had been held to be corrupt in Justice Sinha's judgement in the election case against Indira Gandhi. An amendment was passed to bar the jurisdiction of the courts to consider election disputes concerning the Prime Minister, the President, the Vice-President and the Speaker of the Lok Sabha. It was obvious that the primary objective of this amendment was to provide special protection to the Prime Minister, of a kind unknown in any constitution in the world.[11] To ensure that the validity of the amendment itself was not challenged before the courts a special clause was inserted to place the amendment beyond judicial review. However, the Supreme Court unanimously struck down the provision of the Constitution amendment which prohibited the courts from declaring the election of this special category of persons to be void under the existing law without laying down the law which was to apply to them.

Another factor which is important in this regard was the emergence of the late Sanjay Gandhi, the Prime Minister's younger son as a powerful political figure. It was transpired later that Sanjay was not even a primary member of the Congress party but was nominated as member of the All India Congress Committee (AICC) as well as of the Youth Congress Council, by the then Congress President D.K. Barooah. What was claimed to be "the biggest and quickest peaceful resettlement of people known to history"[12] was started by Sanjay Gandhi, when he forced thousands of slum dwellers out of Delhi. He also led an intensive sterilization drive which included the herding of thousands of unwilling and unmarried people to vasectomy camps. Further he attacked political parties, especially the Community Party of India which he accused as collaborating with the British Raj during independence struggle. To cover and highlight her sons actions, at the Gauhati session of the AICC Indira Gandhi said that an attack on Sanjay was an attack on her.[13] This was perhaps a reference to CPI newspaper "Patriot" which praised Indira Gandhi almost every day but studiously ignored Sanjay Gandhi. Indira Gandhi defended her actions and said that the Emergency had been promulgated to save the country from the opposition's conspiracy to create chaos and confusion.[14] While moving a resolution on 21st July 1976 for approval of Emergency in the Rajya Sabha, Home Minister Bhramananda Reddy said that the incitement of students, army and police by the Sarvodaya leader Jayaprakash Narayan and his friends "could have resulted in a violence of a kind which would have been difficult for the government to control.[15] A similar resolution was moved by Jagjivan Ram in the Lok Sabha, and he congratulated the Prime Minister for having taken "the right action at the right time"[16].

Whatever be the claims of Indira Gandhi and her associates the Emergency of 1975 brought unprecedented peril to the nation and to political leaders, Journalists and public intellectuals opposed to Mrs. Gandhi. Whatever be the immediate causes which led to the Emergency of 1975, basic root of all causes lies mainly in the absence of internal democracy and the developing authoritarian tendencies within the Congress party and the economic crisis which India confronted during the period. The general theoretical interpretation of the causes of dictatorial states can be traced in the words of Jose Maravall. He wrote, firstly the economic crisis, which is related to a threat to the traditional structures of class domination, both are due to a strong working-class movement and to a slump in the process of capital accumulation. A second factor is disaffection of important sections of the ruling class from the existing system of parliamentary democracy. Finally the crisis which forms the background of such states includes situation of political uprootedness among sectors of society that do not participate through the existing channel of political representation and or feel threatened by the social and economic crisis among petty-bourgeoisie, peasantry and lumpen proletariat.[17] In brief the economic crisis which the India was confronting and the rampant corruption among the administrative hierarchy together with authoritarianism and evils of power politics led to the proclamation of Emergency and to the dictatorial rule of Mrs. Gandhi and the Caucus.

Mrs. Gandhi decides to hold Elections

In February 1977, the disputed (Prime Minister and Speaker) Election Ordinance, 1977 was issued. One of the last acts of Mrs. Gandhi's government was to issue on 19th March 1977, necessary rules under this ordinance to complete the process of setting up of a non judicial body to hear petitions challenging the elections of the Prime Minister and the Speaker. With the background of this and the previous laws which the parliament passed during Emergency, Mrs. Gandhi said during the election campaign that "the Prime Minister represents the whole country and any attack on him or her is an attack on the entire population. The abuses being hurled at me by the opposition are tarnishing the image of India".[18] In other words she indirectly held right the Barooah slogan "India is Indira and Indira is India".

Politics would have gone on in this fashion, but Indira Gandhi sprang a surprise on 18th January 1977 by announcing elections to the Lok Sabha. In her unscheduled broadcast to the nation, Mrs. Gandhi, pointed the reason to conduct elections as "to restore the political processes on which we were compelled to put some curbs. We strongly believe that parliamentary government must report back to the people and seek sanction from them to carry out programmes and policies for the nation's strength and welfare".[19] She said that the new election would provide an opportunity to cleanse public eye of confusion. The first reason for proclaiming elections can be traced in the political resolution adopted by the Gauhati session of the AICC on November 21st and 22nd, 1976, which said the "extension of the life of Lok Sabha was clearly in the wider national interests. The overwhelming support of the people that the Congress enjoys would ensure the massive victory of the Congress at the polls at any time; nevertheless, safeguarding the interest of the nation is more important than victory at polls."[20]

The second reason for holding fresh election was that the Intelligence Bureau and the Research Analysis Wing of the cabinet secretariat were bringing stories to the Prime Minister, as opposed to their earlier reports, that she would secure 350 seats if elections were held immediately. Thus, at the end of 1976 the Congress party was sure of its massive victory at the polls at any time. Thirdly there were external pressures also. The Amnesty International, The Socialist International and many other organizations of Indian residents abroad and of foreign nationals were carrying on almost a campaign in the foreign Press that Indira Gandhi had ended all human rights and fundamental freedoms just to stay on power.

Jayaprakash Narayan felt that Mrs. Gandhi had called the elections because she became conscious of the fact that the people of India would not tolerate the Emergency for long and their anger would lead to an explosion.[21] It would be hard to suggest as to which factor was most decisive and it would be more pertinent to conclude that Mrs. Gandhi's decision was the cumulative effect of all the factors above mentioned. Whatever be the factors, for the time being the decision sealed her fate as well as that of the Congress party. The country was launched into a new era.

Formation of Janata Party

Efforts to form a National Opposition party were a decade old. Serious moves were however set a foot only after the split in the Congress party. The so called 'Grand Alliance' of 1971 failed miserably, but finally the Emergency paved the way. The Janata Party, which came into existence soon after the announcement of 1977 Lok Sabha elections was the result of several parties opposed to the Emergency regime, merging together reflected a chartered mood among its politicians. They had gone through a mill of Emergency and hence the first meeting of non-Communist

12

opposition leaders, after Emergency, took place at Bombay which constituted a Steering Committee[22] to draft an 'approach paper' for the opposition parties. They met again on 22-23 May and Jayaprakash Narayan announced the formation of a new party comprising of the Congress (O), Jana Sangh, Bharatiya Lok Dal and the Socialist Party which formally came into being in the last week of June 1976. But due to the unwillingness of certain sections of the Congress (O) the new party did not materialise and this provoked Charan Singh. But the Socialist party, to overcome the inhibitions of Congress (O) in joining a single new party, expressed its willingness to merge itself into Congress (O), provided the party's name was changed something like 'Indian National Socialist Congress'.

Meanwhile changes occurred in the position of Congress (O) and it expressed itself in favour of changes in the party's constitution, so as "to facilitate unification of the democratic opposition parties". Indira Gandhi's announcement about the elections had the effect of immediately brining the Congress (O), Jana Sangh, BLD and the Socialist party together. As Kuldip Nayar writes "the mere instinct to survive had forced the four parties to come together and constitute an electoral party- the Janata Party.[23] In short all other factors, like the insistence of Bharatiya Kranthi Dal and later Bharatiya Lok Dal that merger should be complete, the Jana Sangh attitude that a beginning to be made in the form of concrete action inside legislatures both in Centre and States, a feeling in certain quarters especially of Socialist party that they would not be one ideologically when a united party was established, and the unwillingness of some parties like Congress (O) and the Jana Sangh to dissolve their separate identities, which were prevented the former attempts to merger of the opposition withered away in front of the threat posed by Indira Gandhi's dictatorial rule.

The Janata Party was formally launched in New Delhi on 23rd January,1977 with Morarji Desai as its Chairman and Charan Singh as Deputy Chairman. The party had three General Secretaries - L K Advani and Surendra Mohan, respectively from the erstwhile Jana Sangh and Socialist party and Ram Dhan, former general secretary of the Congress. A National Committee of 37 members[24] were constituted as the top decision-making body. The Janata Party, comprising of the Congress (O), Jana Sangh, BLD, Socialist party and some independent Congressmen accepted the symbol of the BLD – man with a plough and a wheel – as its election symbol.

Many of the leaders of the new party were congressmen who had been a party to many of the actions which gradually led to the erosion of the democratic foundations of the system. Later, in a major political development Jagjivan Ram resigned from the Congress and the Cabinet on 2nd February 1977, to fight for what he called 'decency and integrity' in public eye under the new banner of 'Congress for Democracy', in the Lok Sabha elections.[25] In a joint statement with some other leaders,[26] Jagjivan Ram announced the launching of the Congress for Democracy (CFD). The Janata Party Central Committee on 2nd February passed a resolution which said, "we welcome Jagjivan Ram and all those who have followed him as our valued partners in the mission of saving democracy and restoring national policy on healthy lines."[27] The result was that the leaders of both Janata Party and the CFD immediately came to an electoral understanding on the same symbol of Janata Party. In its Election Manifesto issued on 20th February 1977, CFD described itself as "the revolt of the conscience of the Indian National Congress to preserve and protect the rich traditions and objectives of this great organisation and to carry them forward."[28]

The emergence of Janata party and the Congress for Democracy introduced a new element in Indian politics and this led to the development of election campaign into a war of words between the Congress and the Opposition. L.K. Advani, one of the general secretaries of the Janata party described it as "nation's response to the challenge of totalitarianism that threatens and engulfs the country not just temporarily as has happened already, but forever". Janata party, he said "was not a conglomeration of parties, or a front or an alliance, it is a new national party.[29] Former Congress leader S. Chandrasekhar characterised the new party as a movement that would find new moorings after the elections.[30] On the other hand, while opposing the new party, the CPI General Secretary C. Rajeswara Rao described the Janata party as mainly a new form of the old 1971 reactionary Grand Alliance.[31] Any way he did not criticise the CFD as a reactionary one.

The draft constitution of the Janata party as issued on 29th April, 1977, which interestingly was formed after the party had already been installed into power at the Centre, laid down its objectives as follows; "The Janata party is dedicated to the task of building up a democratic, secular and socialist state in India on Gandhian principles, deriving inspiration from our rich heritage and the noble tradition of our struggle for national independence and individual liberty. The party believes in a policy that ensures decentralization of economic and political power. It affirms the right of peaceful and democratic dissent which includes *satyagraha* or non-violent resistance".[32]

As a final step, meeting in New Delhi on 30th April 1977, the four constituents of the Janata party adopted the resolutions[33] dissolving their parties and approving their merger with the national party which was to come into being in the following day. Meanwhile the demand from the Janata party rank and file for merger of the CFD with the Janata party became increasingly strident. Events did not move in the manner as Jagjivan Ram expected. There were no massive desertions from the Congress party. This helped the merger of the CFD with the Janata Party in the first week of May 1977.

The Janata party formally launched its inaugural convention at Pragati Maidan, New Delhi, on 1st May 1977. After its inaugural session, the party chose S. Chandrasekhar as the new president of the party, in place of Morarji Desai, who became Prime Minister of India. Thus, the emergence of formidable new party even though short lived on the Indian political scene was completed.

Notes and References:

1   G.G. Mirchandani, 32 *Million Judges*, New Delhi, 1977, p.5.

2   V.K. Narasimhan, *Democracy Redeemed*, New Delhi, 1977, p.1.

3   Rajni Kothari, 'Delivery Goods', *Seminar*, No. 242, October, 1979, p.16.

4   Bashiruddhin Ahamed, 'The Crisis of Change', *Seminar* No. 242, October 1979, p.25.

5   *Ibid*. p.26.

6   *The Indian Express*, 25 June, 1975.

7   *Ibid*

8   Mohan Ram, 'The Key Issue', *Economic and Political Weekly*, Vol. XII, No.6, 7, 8 Annual Number 1977, p. 175.

9   D.C. Gupta, *Indian Government and Politics*, New Delhi, 1979, p. 653.

10 The Organizations include: R.S.S, Jama at-Islami, Anand Marge and several CPI (M.L.) groups (Naxalites).

11 V.K. Narasimhan, *Democracy Redeemed*, p. 13.

12 G.G.Mirchandani, *32 Million Judges*, p. 71.

13 *The Indian Express*, 22 November 1976.

14 *The Indian Express*, 27 June 1977.

15 *The Times of India*, 22 July 1975.

16 *Ibid*

17 *The Hindu*, 21 February, 1977.

18 *The Hindu*, 21 February, 1977.

19 *The Indian Express*, 19 January, 1977.

20 *Ibid*. 23 November, 1976.

21 *The Statesman*, 18 February, 1977.

22 The Steering Committee consisted of Shanti Bhushan, H.M. Patel, O.P. Tyagi and N.G. Gorey.

23 Kuldip Nayar. *The Judgement*, New Delhi, 1977, p. 161.

24 The National Committee includes opposition leaders like Ashok Mehta, A.B. Vajpayee, Bhanu Pratap Singh, B.S. Shekhawat, Biju Patnaik, C.B. Gupta, Chand Ram, Chandrasekhar, H.M. Patel, P.C. Sen, N.G. Gorey, N. Sanjiva Reddy, Nanaji Deshmuk, Mrs. Mrinal Gorey, Samar Guha, Sikandar Bakht, P. Ramachandran, Karpoor Takur and Shahti Bhushan (Treasurer).

25 *The Hindu*, 3 February, 1977.

26 The Co-signatories to the joint statement were: H.N. Bahuguna, Nadini Satpathy, K.R. Ganesh, D.N. Tiwari and Raj Mangel Panday.

27 *The Indian Express*, 3 February, 1977.

28 *Ibid.* 21, February, 1977.

29 *Ibid.* 30 March, 1977.

30 *The Hindu*, 15 March, 1977.

31 *Ibid.* 17 March, 1977.

32 Sachidanand Sinha, *The Permanent Crisis in India: After Janata What?* New Delhi, 1978 p.4.

33 The resolutions were moved by A. B. Vajpayee, Raj Narain, Babubhai Patel and N.G. Gorey respectively for Jana Sangh, BLD, Cong (O) and the Socialist Party.

3

The 1977 Lok Sabha Elections: Democracy Revisited

Political sociologists Robert Dowse and John Hughes views elections as one type of social mechanism amongst others for aggravating preferences of a particular kind.[1] Elections provide the means for the peaceful and orderly transfer of power, for dealing with the vexing problem of succession, for the routinisation of political change. In Michael Brecher's words "Elections become a non-violent way of solving a difficulty common to all political systems- how to organise the succession from one group of men holding authority to another."[2] Elections provide the occasion for the widest degree of popular participation. They constitute the most important single arena for genuine competition between political groups. They are the principal agencies through which recruitment to a significant part of the political elite is affected. Through the election even the ordinary village man comes to share the democratic experience of the country.

India's sixth national election to parliament was transformed by the events of the Emergency to a referendum. On a single issue- would Indians give the Congress party a mandate to continue the form of dictatorship established by Indira Gandhi in June 1975 or would they choose to return to rule of law and the restoration of civil and political liberties. Of an electorate of 320 million, roughly sixty percent voted the new party to power, reducing the Congress for the first time since independence to a minority. It was Indira Gandhi who unwittingly gave birth to the Janata party and it was the people, the "sleeping Leviathan"[3] of India, who suddenly rose in a mass upsurge with the Janata flag as its crest.

Electoral Alliances

Mrs. Gandhi dissolved the fifth Lok Sabha before fifteen months of its term is due expire.[4] The first and most immediate development that took place in the country after Indira Gandhi's decision, as pointed out earlier, was the Emergency with all its concomitant abuses, excesses and atrocities, that created a situation in which the fragmented opposition had no choice but to come together. The Emergency imposed on 25th June 1975 was relaxed, still the March 1977 poll was held with a double emergency in force.[5]

Unlike the earlier elections to Lok Sabha, in the 1977 elections, there has been a polarisation of the main political parties. The coming together of the opposition parties for the sixth Lok Sabha elections is qualitatively different. In the 1971 elections there originated the 'Grand Alliance', but the parties who joint together on that occasion contested the elections with separate symbols and separate manifestos, different from the emergence of Janata Party in 1977. In 1977, the coming together of the opposition compelled the component units to leave atleast for the period some of their ideas, as a compromise for the emergence of a new party and for their own survival.

After the 'coming together' the Janata Party joined hands with the Akali Dal in Punjab, and the Dravida Munnetta Kazhagam (DMK) in Tamil Nadu.[6] The Communist Party of India (Marxist) declared that it shares the Janata Party's views on Emergency, on the 42nd Constitution Amendment and the role of judiciary. But it would not join the new party because of its ideological and class interests. It has declared itself in favour of electoral adjustments with the Janata Party to avoid splitting the non- Congress vote[7] and also hold the view that without civil liberties no economic progress was possible.

As against the Opposition, the Congress also looked for allies and found them in the Communist Party of India and All India Anna Dravida Mennetta Kazhagam of Tamil Nadu. While the CPI

19

supported the Emergency regime of Mrs. Gandhi, her son Sanjay Gandhi did not want to have anything to do with the CPI, against which he had launched a campaign. But Mrs. Gandhi reassured him that the alliance would be only on Congress terms.[8] The CPI stand was mainly in line with the pro-Congress attitude of the Soviet Union. Congress also made an alliance with the National Conference in Jammu and Kashmir.

Manifestos-Emphasis on Political Issues

The outstanding difference between the Congress manifesto and those of all other parties including the CPI, lay in the way each looked at the National Emergency. The Congress manifesto released on 8th February asserted "the commitment of the Congress to democracy is absolute, irrevocable and unshakable".[9] But it failed to explain why the extraordinary powers that the government armed itself with during the Emergency should continue. The manifesto has defended the imposition of emergency to save the country from what it called a catastrophe and upheld the constitutional amendments with the argument that the party was well within its right to remove the obstacles placed by vested interests in the way of socio-economic transformation.

The Janata Party manifesto qualified the election as the most crucial that the country had since independence. It declared the choice before the people as a choice between "freedom and slavery", between "democracy and dictatorship".[10] The manifesto called the Emergency as a "nightmare of fear and humiliation".[11] It condemned the 42nd amendment to the Constitution as concentration of power and pointed to the Press censorship as an instrument of the reign of terror. The manifesto contained a nineteen-number political charter.[12] The CFD manifesto has the imprint of a new party just born, and tried to find its feet. It said that the CFD stands for a modern India of the vision of Jawaharlal Nehru.[13]

The CPI manifesto envisaged the electoral strategy of the CPI as an adjustment with the Congress in some states and in others a tilt towards the Congress for Democracy. It ruled out any arrangement with the Janata Party. The manifesto does not denounce Emergency unreservedly as the CPI (M) and Janata party did, although it wanted it lifted. In contrast to the CPI manifesto, the CPI(M) manifesto released on 31st January is with full of bitterness against the Congress, the Emergency and the 42nd Constitution amendment. It said that the election will be held under the Emergency and the 'so called relaxation' is only a 'show piece' to deceive the people and the world".[14]

As regards the social and economic policies, the Congress manifesto, while reaffirming its firm commitment to fully implement the 25 point programme, promised to continue its crusade against untouchability. It promised to work unremittingly to raise the living standards of the Scheduled Castes and Scheduled Tribes to remove economic and social discrimination against women and to end the evil of dowry system.[15] The most surprising omission in the Congress manifesto is the role of the multinationals in the economy of the country. The Janata Party had a thirteen-point economic charter,[16] one of which calls for the deletion of property as a fundamental right. It also contained a fifteen-point social charter.[17] The CFD manifesto was broadly on the terms of the Janata Party's programme. Like the Janata the CFD said that bonus is a deferred wage.[18]

The basic economic policies of the two Communist parties is almost the same. Both the CPI and the CPI(M) have demanded nationalisation of textile, jute, sugar, cement and foreign drug industries and the takeover of the whole-sale trade. The CPI(M) manifesto said that the Congress had mismanaged the economy in order to serve the interests of monopolists and land lords.[19] It urged the abolition of landlordism, the complete takeover of foreign capital and a ban on multinational companies. Both the CPI and the CPI(M) have demanded the right to collective bargaining and the right to strike. For the first time in an Indian election, family planning is a contentious issue in the March 1977 poll. This is because of the widespread allegations of coercion, intimidation and forcible sterilisation to achieve family planning targets during Emergency.

21

Foreign affairs did not receive the same prominence in 1977 manifestos as in earlier ones. There is little difference in approach among major parties. The Congress and the Janata, both were against colonialism. The Congress has pledged to adhere to Non-alignment "which has kept India out of military blocs", while the Janata party is for "genuine non-alignment"[20] free from any attachment to any power blocs. The Communist parties again emphasised the struggle against imperialism. While the CPI (M) expressed its happiness in the improvement of relations with China, the CPI manifesto had not mentioned about it.

Election Campaign[21]

The sixth Lok Sabha election was the most exciting held in India so far. The Opposition was united as never before. In no previous elections issues of economic, social, foreign and defence policies been relegated so far to the background as in the 1977 election. In a sense, therefore the election really became a battle for the recovery of democratic freedoms, although other local issues or grievances might have influenced the voters in certain areas.

The curtain lifted with Indira Gandhi's surprise broadcast on January 18, 1977, regarding the fresh election. Beginning in a subdued form the Opposition campaign acquired a boost after Jagjivan Ram's resignation from the Congress party, attacking the exercise of official power by a "small coterie or an individual" which everyone understood to refer Sanjay Gandhi. The Opposition put the choice before the people- whether they wanted "democracy or dictatorship". While pointing to the emergence of Sanjay Gandhi as a powerful centre of power, they said that Mrs. Gandhi attempted to found a dynasty. To this the Congress answer was a counter question whether people wanted "democracy or disruption" and condemned Jagjivan Ram's exit as one of individual defection.

It was Jayaprakash Narayan the advocate of 'Total Revolution' and the main architect of the Janata Party, provided the focus to Opposition. He requested the masses to bring the Janata Party into power. He said, " this is the last chance, if you falter, nineteen months of tyranny shall become nineteen years of terror".[22] All opposition parties including the CFD talked of extra constitutional centres of power. Their views on the issues like the emergency, constitutional amendments and related matters have interesting nuances. JP and other leaders of Opposition had spoken of inhuman excesses that had been committed during Emergency. Adding strength to the opposition campaign, the People's Union for Civil Liberties adopted a resolution which said that in many respects. "The 42nd amendment of the constitution has institutionalised the suppression of civil liberties and democratic rights in our country.[23]

While the Janata party could draw upon a number of front rank leaders to carry on its election campaign, including Jayaprakash Narayan and Acharya Kripalani, the election campaign for the Congress had to be conducted almost entirely by Indira Gandhi. It was indeed remarkable that she bore the burden of this campaign with boundless energy. She stressed that the Janata Party was not different from the "Grand Alliance" of 1971 and emphasised on the economic gains of Emergency. She herself asked the people "to forget and forgive" and stressed the importance of a 'strong centre' and 'political stability".[24] She attacked Janata Party as a "hotchpotch", anti-Muslim as it includes Rashtriya Swayam Sevak Sangh (RSS) and claimed that the only party which could look after the interests of minorities is the Congress. In brief the campaign as a whole was remarkable exercise in the political education on the world's largest electorate among whom most of them are illiterate.

Indira Gandhi and the Congress Faced the Crusade

As pointed out earlier India's sixth national election to parliament was transformed by the events of Emergency to a referendum which resulted in the rout of the Congress party out of office by the Janata Party and other opposition parties. By and large the elections were a great victory for the Indian people. By their verdict for the first time since independence, the ruling Congress party was swept out of power and its leader and Prime Minister Indira Gandhi was defeated decisively by over 55, 200 votes at the hands of her old rival Raj Narain at Rae Bareli in Uttar Pradesh. In the neighbouring Amethi constituency Sanjay Gandhi, perhaps the most controversial figure emerged on the political scene during Emergency was also defeated by the Janata Party candidate by 75,844 votes. Two thirds of the nineteen members of the council of ministers, who represented the Emergency regime and contested the elections were defeated.

The defeat of the Congress was quite dismal. It managed to muster only 153 seats as against 350 in the 1971 elections. The Janata Party and its ally, the CFD won 298 seats. The Congress did not get a single seat in Uttar Pradesh, Bihar, Haryana, Punjab and Delhi. While the Janata swept the north, it did seep through the Vindhyas. It won one seat in each Andhra Pradesh, Tamil Nadu and Karnataka. As regards to the two Communist parties which contested the elections, the CPI which was in alliance with the Congress was badly mauled. It ended up with just seven seats against 23 in 1971. The CPI (M) won 22 seats as against 25 in 1971. The tragic fact which the CPI (M) confronted in the 1977 elections was that it electorally wiped out in Kerala, one of its two traditional strongholds.

'The Indian Express' daily greeted the electorate's verdict and wrote "historians of democracy would perhaps record the decisive verdict of the Indian people in the sixth Lok Sabha elections as marking democracy's finest hour. The average Indian voter has demonstrated maturity in exercising his franchise and has taught a lesson to rulers who might be inclined to take him for granted as a passive and pliable pawn in the game of power politics".[25] 'The Hindu', qualified it as the greatest electoral upset in India's political history.[26] The world press hailed the verdict. The largest circulated paper the 'New York Daily News' said that "totalitarian rule took a deserved drubbing from the voters".[27] 'The London Times' views it as the "fall of the Nehru Dynasty".[28] China voiced its pleasure at the defeat of the Congress party, while the Soviet newspaper, 'Izvestia' attributed the defeat to "mistakes and excesses" committed after the introduction of Emergency.[29]

Table 3. I

1977 March Lok Sabha Election: Seats Contested and Won

States/Union Territories	Seats	Congress		Janata		CPI		CPI(M)		Others		Independents	
		C	W*	C	W	C	W	C	W	C		C	W
1	2	3	4	5	6	7	8	9	10	11	12	13	14
Andhra Pradesh	42	42	41	37	1	10	8	6	–	3	–	67	–
Assam	14	14	10	11	3	2	–	–	–	3	–	9	1
Bihar	54	54	–	52	52	22	–	2	–	24	1	86	1
Gujarat	26	26	10	26	16	–	–	–	–	–	–	60	–
Haryana	10	9	–	10	10	2	–	1	–	–	–	24	–
Himachal Pradesh	4	4	–	4	3	1	–	1	–	(VHP) 3	1	4	–
Jammu & Kashmir	6	3	2	2	–	–	–	National Congress	–	3	3	21	1
Karnataka	28	28	26	28	2	3	–	–	–	1	–	37	–
Kerala	20	11	11	2	–	4	4	9	–	10	5	26	–
Madhya Pradesh	40	38	1	39	37	3	–	–	–	1	1	72	1
Maharashtra	48	47	20	30	19	4	–	4	3	(PWP 7+6)	5	108	1
Manipur	2	2	2	2	–	2	–	–	–	2	–	3	–

States/Union Territories	Seats	Congress		Janata		CPI		CPI(M)		Others		Independents	
		C	W*	C	W	C	W	C	W	C		C	W
1	2	3	4	5	6	7	8	9	10	11	12	13	14
Meghalaya	2	2	1	-	-	-	-	-	-	1	1	5	-
Nagaland	1	1	-	-	-	-	-	-	-	1	1	-	-
Orissa	21	20	4	20	15	5	-	1	1	3	-	12	1
Punjab	13	13	-	12	3	6	-	1	1	(AKaliDal) 9+5	8+1	45	-
Rajasthan	25	25	1	24	24	3	-	2	-	1	-	47	-
Sikkim	1	1	1	-	-	-	-	-	-	-	-	-	-
Tamilnadu	39	15	14	18	3	3	3	2	(DMK) (AIADMK)	19	1	116	-
Tripura	2	2	1	1	1	1	-	2	-	37	18	3	-
Uttar Pradesh	85	85	-	85	85	13	-	20	-	-	-	257	-
West Bengal	42	34	3	15	15	3	-	-	17	1	-	79	1
Andamans	1	1	1	1	-	-	-	-	-	15	6	-	-
Arunachal Pradesh	2	2	1	-	-	-	-	-	-	-	-	2	1
Chandigarh	1	1	-	1	1	1	-	-	-	-	-	7	-
D & N Haveli	1	1	1	1	-	-	-	-	-	-	-	1	-

States/Union Territories	Seats	Congress		Janata		CPI		CPI(M)		Others		Independents	
		C	W*	C	W	C	W	C	W	C	W	C	W
1	2	3	4	5	6	7	8	9	10	11	12	13	14
Delhi	7	7	-	7	7	1	-	-	-	1	-	25	-
Goa, Daman & Diu	2	2	1	2	-	-	-	-	(MGP)	2	-	9	-
Lakshadweep	1	1	1	-	-	-	-	-	-	-	1	1	-
Mizoram	1	1	-	-	-	-	-	-	-	2	-	1	-
Pondicherry	1	-	-	1	-	-	-	-	(AIADMK)	1	1		1
Total	542	492	153	422	297	91	7	54	22	145	54	1222	9

* Seats contested and Seats won.

Source: G.G.Mirchandani, 32 Million Judges, (New Delhi, 1977), p.158.

Following the defeat of the Congress party, Indira Gandhi tendered the resignation letter to acting President B.D. Jatti and said "the collective judgement of the people must be respected. My colleagues and I accepted this verdict unreservedly and in a spirit of humility".[30]

Factionalism within the Congress, the resignation of Jagjivan Ram and his associates, the suppression of working class and the disenchantment of the middle class with the ruling party, the high handedness displayed by functionaries of the government and ruling party following the declaration of Emergency, the towering personality of Jayaprakash Narayan who had emerged almost as a father figure on the national scene along with the open support of Shahi Imam of Delhi to the Janata - CFD combine contributed for making the death-knell of the Congress party in the 1977 parliamentary elections. The Emergency excesses angered every section of the people the peasants, the landless the urban poor, state employees, small traders and all others who formed the Congress social base turned against it. The vote against the Congress was thus a vote of anger against authoritarianism and highhandedness. In this sense the votes which the opposition gained in 1977 Lok Sabha elections were negative in character.

It is apparently clear that Indira Gandhi, her Congress and her Emergency regime were not only unpopular, but hated by a considerable proportion of the people. In the circumstances the votes she did get were probably out of old loyalties to the Nehru family and because of the Nehru charisma.[31] Whether this statement was correct or not, the thundering victory of the opposition, which fought on the plank of democracy and freedom came as a great surprise to the intelligentsia in India and the people in the west. Little did they realise that the poor loved their liberty as much as anybody else. Their approach might not have been so sophisticated or ideologically pure but their faith in what they considered democracy was unfliching. The poor illiterate and semi-illiterate masses have the first time made their voice felt on the issue of political liberty. They voted the Janata in so that liberal freedoms and rights could be restored.[32] And the credit mainly goes to them to have liberated a demoralised and disoriented elite that had abandoned the very ground which fostered its chief claim to the leadership of the nation.

The election made the history for other reasons also. The Janata Party which defeated the Congress was inspired and led by the most unusual figure in Indian politics since Mahathma Gandhi- Jayaprakash Narayan. JP's return to national prominence restored the breath of idealism to the political controversy and revived echoes of an age of grand striving still fresh in Indian memory.[33] Further the election revived two political processes stunted by Indira Gandhi's style and the techniques of governing party and country: the natural development of the post Nehru leadership within the Congress, and the natural development of an Opposition as a growing challenge to Congress. The myth of indispensability was quietly disposed of at the polls and a path opened for a new, perhaps unknown leadership of the Congress.

It is clear from the entire context that the upper class elite combination in India which wanted to use Indira Gandhi as the most appropriate agent to subserve their interests.[34] The defeat of Indira Gandhi in the political field did not end the danger of dictatorship because faced with popular threat to its privileges the upper class elitist complex may find other agents to take over her mantle. However, the 1977 Lok Saba election's immediate achievement was the restoration of a legitimate political process, more important in the long run than the question of whether the coalition it had brought to power survived or not.

Notes and References:

1   Robert E. Dowse and John A. Hughes, *Political Sociology* , London, p. 382.

2   Norman D. Palmer, *Elections and Political Development* , New Delhi, 1975, p. 52.

3   Janardan Takur, *All the Janata Men* , New Delhi, 1978, p.3.

4   The life of the Lok Sabha extended twice during the period, on 4 February, 1976, and on 5 November 1976, for one year each time.

5   The external Emergency declared on 3 December 1974 in the wake of Bangladesh was and the Internal Emergency declared on June 25, 1975, were withdrawn on 27 March 1979, by the Janata government.

6   In Tamil Nadu and Pondicherry, the Janata party contested the elections with the symbol of Congress (o) and not on the symbol of BLD.

7   *The Hindu*, 7 February, 1977.

8   Kuldip Nayar, *The Judgement*, p.164.

9   S.L. Shakdher (ed.), *The Sixth General Elections to Lok Sabha*, New Delhi, 1977, p. 62.

10 *Election Manifesto of Janata party*, New Delhi 1997.

11 *Ibid.*

12 See Appendix - 1.

13 *The Indian Express*, 1 February, 1977.

14 S.L. Shakdar (Ed.), *The Sixth General Elections to Lok Sabha*, p. 50.

15 *Link*, 13 February, 1977, p. 11.

16 See Appendix - 1.

17 S.L.Shakdhar (Ed.), *The Sixth General Election to Lok Sabha*, p. 78.

18 See Appendix-1

19 Mohan Ram, 'Janata Party Portents', *Economic and Political Weekly of India*, 29 January 1977, p. 27.

20 The idea of genuine Non-alignment is based on the view that India's foreign policy then was pro-soviet. But in practice the protagonists of 'genuine non-alignment' tried in vain to give it a pro-American, pro-western orientation due to international compulsions.

21 The idea of genuine Non-alignment is based o the view that India's foreign policy then was pro-soviet. But in practice the protagonists of 'genuine non-alignment' tried to vain to give it a pro-American, pro-western orientation due to international compulsions.

22 *The Statesman*, 28 February, 1977.

23 *The Hindu*,14, March 1977.

24 *The Hindu*, 6 February, 1977.

25 *The Indian Express*, 22 March, 1977.

26 *The Hindu*, 22 March, 1977.

27 S.L.Shakdher, *The Sixth General Election to Lok Sabha*

28 *Ibid.*

29 *Ibid.*

30 *The Hindu*, 24 March, 1977.

31 K.A. Abbas, *20 March 1977 A Day like and Other day*, New Delhi, 1978, p.120.

32. K. Raghavendra Rao, 'Understanding the Indian State: A Historical-Materialist Exercise', in Zoya Hasan, et al., The State, Political Process, and Identity: Reflections on Modern India, New Delhi, Sage Publications,1989, p.94.

32 Nayantara Saihgal, *Indira Gandhi's Emergence and Style*, New Delhi, 1978, p. 208.

33 Sachchidanand Sinha, *Ergency in Perspective; Reprieve and challenge*, Delhi, 1977, p. 116.

4

Politics After The Poll: Fragmentation and Instability

In the history of modern India an era ended with the defeat of the Congress Party and it's leader Indira Gandhi. It was neither white nor black. Mrs. Gandhi's efforts to keep the country together was by no standard a mean contribution. She showed courage in espousing India's foreign policy of Non-Alignment in world forums. In political matters she took the path which most would fear to tread fighting can't and convention. But courage was no substitute for good deeds or for the methods employed to achieve them. This had been the strongest and the weakest point in Indira Gandhi's tenure as Prime Minister of India, which ultimately led to the defeat of the Congress party and loss of power.

Janata Forms the Government

The sixth Lok Sabha was duly constituted on March 23[rd]1977 through a notification of the Election Commission of India.[1] Backed by the 297 members of the Janata party and the CFD and supported by eight Akali Dal members, twenty two CPI (M) members and a nineteen other members, Morarji Desai became Prime Minister of India. He was sworn into office on March 24th, by the Acting President B.D. Jatti. The process of electing the leader for Prime Ministership was handled by Jayaprakash Narayan and Acharya Kripalani. The CFD expected that their leader Jagjivan Ram should have been elected for premiership. Consequently, the process of building up consensus within the Janata party and the CFD was mishandled. Jagjivan Ram announced that the Congress for Democracy would remain as a separate organisation within the Parliament and outside and would extend support to the Janata party government.[2] But the misgivings between the partners were sorted out with the intervention of JP. Consequently, CFD merged in the Janata party and its leaders joined Morarji Desai's government. It was the end of the chapter in the ministerial drama, but the curtain has not yet rung because for the CFD it was a "breach of faith all along the line" for the Janata Party, it was "dictation by the other side".

Developments within the Congress Party

Whenever there is instability and confusion in Indian politics, the Indian National Congress becomes its victim. In its chequered career of a century, this great national organisation has faced many crises, including three splits. After its formation in 1885 the first crisis that the Congress faced was at Surat in 1907, between moderates and extremists. The split was in a way the harbinger of the common people's involvement in Congress affairs, which until then was dominated by the educated elite.[3] The second split occurred at the Tripuri session in 1939, when Subhas Chandra Bose was elected as the Congress president, defeating Mahatma Gandhi's nominee, Dr. Pattabhi Sitaramayya. Gandhi was adamant and refused to cooperate with Subhas Bose. Hence Bose resigned from the Congress presidentship and left the Congress with his supporters and formed the All India Forward Bloc.

The split in 1969 was however the most serious in the annals of the Congress. It came about the Bangalore AICC session in July 1969. The rift took the form of an economic policy entitled "Stray Thoughts" and finally led to the defeat of Sanjiva Reddi, the official candidate of the Congress for the presidentship of India. V.V. Giri became president of India with the support of Indira Gandhi and the leftists. The 1969 split led to a polarisation of Indian politics that more accurately reflected the basic policy differences among its ideologically divided leaders.[4]

Once power was gone out of the hands of the congressmen they began to quarrel among themselves and accusations and counter accusations and allegations and counter allegations began. Thus Y.B. Chavan, who was to be the leader of the opposition in the new Lok Sabha and who did not utter a word against Emergency during its operation for nineteen months, denounced emergency and indicted Indira Gandhi, for her regime during that period. On 27th March, 125 Congress Members of Parliament and State legislative assemblies demanded the expulsion of the of the "caucus of four"[5] from the party.[6] In the Congress Working Committee, which met on 11th April, the role of the clique close to Mrs. Gandhi was decried most by those who were the supporters of emergency regime earlier. Sidhartha Sankar Ray and Shah Nawaz Khan were in the forefront among these critics. Meanwhile in a letter circulated, A.K. Antony took the position that, had Indira Gandhi relinquished the Prime Ministership after the Allahabad High Court verdict, setting aside her election to the Lok Sabha. He conceded that nobody can find fault with Indira Gandhi for taking that decision of not resigning at that time. He believed that the people like him, who on hearing the news of the judgement sent messages, crying her to continue in office as Prime Minister, are guilty of self-betrayal if they start blaming others for what happened.[7] The working committee expelled Bansilal from the party for a period of six years for his undemocratic and in dignified activities which had damaged the party. The meeting also decided to reprimand V.C. Shukla, formerly Minister of Information and Broadcasting, on a charge of misuse or power.[8]

The Congress President D.K. Barooah resigned from that office on 12th April and stood condemned on all sides. Swaran Singh, the new provisional president, stressed on collective leadership. Indira Gandhi unreservedly owned up full responsibility for her party's defeat and on 2nd May she said, she would "keep out of politics for sometimes."[9] Meanwhile the group of 'Congressmen for Socialist Unity' was formed and its leaders, H.D. Malaviya and N.N. Nanda declared that they stand for "touch with the people," which was lost under Emergency. According to them in Congress "adhocism became the rule and unwanted leaders were forced on the organisational structure".[10]

On 4th and 5th May, the AICC met in New Delhi to examine the causes of party debacle in the elections, in which T.A. Pai, Priyaranjan Das Munshi and Thulasi Dasappa made oblistering attacks on Sanjay Gandhi and the men around him ran the affairs of the nation during emergency.[11] Sidhartha Sankar Ray contested against Indira Gandhi's nominee to the Congress presidentship - Brahmanand Reddy, but lost the contest. Later in statement issued on 12th May, four leaders[12] of the Congress called for an end to their "pathetic and often pathological dependence on an individual" - Indira Gandhi, the still lingering habits of deification and rejection and exposure of the politics of the marionettes and wire pullers.[13]

The supporters of Indira Gandhi started lobbying to ensure her to play a dominant role in the Congress affairs. They wanted Mrs. Gandhi to be consulted on all major decisions taken by the Congress President and the leader of the Congress Parliamentary Party. However, Y.B. Chavan and Brahmanand Reddy rejected this interpretation of the concept of collective leadership. Meanwhile Indira Gandhi was arrested by the CBI on charges of corruption and misuse of power for personal ends on 31st October 1977. But she was released by the court on the ground that there were no grounds for believing that the accusations against her were well founded. The manner in which the whole business was carried out put the Janata government ridicule and won for Indira Gandhi a measure of sympathy among the people.

During the same period, the Shah Commission was appointed and started its functioning. Several former Ministers[14] and officials pointed Indira Gandhi and her son for the misdeeds of Emergency. Factors like this brought home to Mrs. Gandhi that her safety and survival depended upon rebuilding her political image. So from the first she chose to defame Shah Commission, to accuse it of partisanship and to challenge its authority to sit in judgement over her actions as Prime Minister. Secondly, she understood the importance and necessity of the recapturing of the Congress party apparatus and started politics of manipulation. In her struggle Indira Gandhi was supported by Kamalpati Thripati, K.C. Pant, A.R. Antuley and Devaraj Urs.

Meanwhile the Congress performed somewhat better in 1977 assembly elections than what it had done in March 1977. There was some indication that there was growing disillusionment with the Janata Party. However, the infighting within the Congress had its repercussions in state politics, especially in Karnataka. The decision of Devaraj Urs, the then Chief Minister of Karnataka to set up a commission of inquiry to investigate the charge of corruption against K.H. Patil and some others resulted in the disciplinary action against Urs by the Congress Working Committee. This led to split in the Working Committee and on 10th December, Indira Gandhi left the AICC headquarters in support of Mr. Devaraj Urs.[15]

Matters went ahead when Indira Gandhi resigned from the Congress Working Committee on 18th December and her seven supporters[16] on 27th of the same month. Those who backed Indira Gandhi called for a convention on new year day in 1978 in which Mrs. Gandhi said that the Congress High Command had only one aim, to keep her out and denigrate her leadership. On 2nd January 1979 the Congress split and the convention unanimously passed a resolution electing Indira Gandhi as president of the new born party- Indian National Congress (Indira).[17]The rhetoric of mutually hostile exchanges between the two factions of the Congress on the eve of and since the split would suggest that four issues underlie it[18] - the emergency, the influence of the caucus, inner party democracy and collective leadership.

While commenting on the split Y.B. Chavan said, "the Janata party should thank god that she has not declared herself as prime minister".[19] Priyaranjan Das Munshi, the Youth Congress leader, reacted bitterly and said, "the cancer is out, pure blood can now be pumped in".[20] For the Congress the split was something of a traumatic experience and the New Year began with a disturbing uncertainty regarding alignment of forces in the country. Before examining the impact of the split, it is relevant here to look into the later developments which took place between the two Congress parties and also within the Indira Congress in a nutshell.

Following the split some important leaders of the Congress have continued to talk of unity with the Congress (I), which spread confusion in the ranks. As a result every effort of Congressmen to distinguish themselves from the Congress (I) or to project the party as a viable political entity has remained half hearted. Meanwhile within hours of her being declared guilty of committing breach of privilege and contempt of Lok Sabha by the Privileges Committee of the House, Indira Gandhi made a call for unity. Reacting to her call and facing with firm opposition, the Congress Working Committee on 24th November adopted a resolution for exploring the possibility of bringing about "unity among Congressmen under the banner of Indian National Congress, keeping in mind the objectives and programmes and the necessity for democratic functioning of the party."[21] It is true that the basic motivation of the two parties in joining hands was their joint anxiety to capture power. Fortunately, during this time Indira Gandhi and Devaraj Urs finally parted and a dramatic new phase emerged in the Indian political scene. This new phase put an end to the unity talks. The breakdown of the tortuous unity talks between the Indian National Congress and the Indira Congress has at last convinced even the most timid and well meaning Congress leaders that the exercise was a futile one and must be permanently abandoned.

What ultimately swung Indira Gandhi to move against Devaraj Urs was his attack at the AICC (I) session in Delhi on 21st April, on those attempting to rehabilitate her son in party politics, and his threat that unless such attempts were not given up he would begin exposing all such persons in public. Events reached on higher scales when on 8th June 1979, Congress (I) Parliamentary Board resolved that Urs should quit the Karnataka PCC presidentship. In opposition the Karnataka district congress committee chiefs met in Bangalore on 10th June and expressed themselves in favour of Devaraj Urs. The Congress (I) dissolved the Karanataka PCC and appointed Bangarappa, the P W D Minister in the Urs Cabinet as the new adhoc PCC chief. Consequently, Devaraj Urs formed his own party known as the Karnataka Congress[22] which later merged in the Congress. Thus, one of the most durable political partnerships had come to an end.

When the news of the Indira-Urs split became more or less official, N. Tirpunde, the leader of the Congress (I) legislature party and virtual leader of the State unit of Maharashtra, vehemently criticised Sanjay Gandhi and demanded that Mrs. Gandhi's son be thrown out of the Congress(I) and added "Devaraj Urs is the latest victim of Sanjay".[23] A.K.Antony, the Congress leader from Kerala, said in an interview that "the measures which Indira leadership meted out to counter advocates of internal democracy like Devaraj Urs will open the eyes of all Congress supporters.[24] The ouster of Urs is not difficult to understand. Throughout the eighteen months after the Congress split in January 1978, he had functioned independently in his home state, refusing to submit either to Mrs. Gandhi's dictates or pressures.

Indira Gandhi and her supporters opted the split in the Congress because they calculated that the Congress Party headed by Bhramanand Reddi would pursue its policy of constructive co-operation with Janata government to such an extend that it will get identified with the Janata party and alienated from the weaker sections of the people. They felt that with her 'socialist image' Indira Gandhi will offer an alternative to the weaker sections who will otherwise be forced to move towards the Leftist parties. The basic assumption in this line is that the Janata party is a rightist party that will pursue policies against the interests of the weaker sections. And with its support to the Janata government, the Congress headed by Bhramanand Reddy will also get a rightist image. But things happened not fully as expected by the Indira Congress leadership due to unexpected circumstances which we may analyse in the following chapter. Thus, within eighteen months of breaking away from the Congress, Indira Gandhi had split her own party with the obvious aim of suppressing all remaining sources of dissent in her camp.

Fragmentation Spreads to Other Parties

The fragmentation of political parties was not confined to the Congress only. The Akali Dal in Punjab, despite its religious obscurantism was split into two groups - the Talwandi group and the Badal group and the Akali Takt played a major role.

The National Conference of Kashmir was split into Sheiksh Abdulla's majority faction and Mirza Beg's minority faction. The Maharashtravadi Gomanthak Party of Goa and the AIADMK of Tamil Nadu also faced factionalism. Within the Communist Party of India also differences emerged with S.A. Dange demanding support to Indira Gandhi as the representative of the national bourgeoisie and C. Rajeswara Rao and the majority of party leaders and workers advocating Leftist unity. Even the Congress headed by Y. B. Chavan, as we seen earlier, had two groups-one favouring and independent stand and the other led by Swaran Singh and others demanding merger of Congress parties. Thus, except the CPI (M) all other parties faced fragmentation and split during the period.

In short the split in the Congress had far reaching implications for Indian democracy and the future of party system. After the elections of March 1977 there was just a hope that the Two Party System would become a possibility with the Communist Parties functioning as a third force exerting pressure on the government. But the process of polarisation confronted a sudden opposition with the Congress split. Secondly, it also had an effect on the Janata party which was threatening to fall into pieces even before it has had time to consolidate its desperate elements and the differences among its leaders. The breakup of the Congress hastened the process of widening the gulf within the different elements of the Janata Party.

Notes and References:

1   *The Hindu*, 24 March, 1977.

2   *Ibid* 24 March, 1977.

3   Rafil Zakaria; 'The Congress', *Illustrated Weekly of India*, 29 January-4 February, 1979, p.14.

4   Stanley Wolper: *A New History of India*, New York, 1977, p. 393.

5   The so called 'caucus of four' were-Sanjay Gandhi, Bansilal, V.C. Shukla and Om Mehta.

6   *The Hindustan Times,* 12 April 1977.

39

7   *Link,* 17 April 1977.

8   *The Statesman,* 17 April 1977.

9   *The Indian Express, 3 May 1977.*

10 *Ibid.,* 17 April 1977.

11 *Ibid.,* 6 May 1977.

12 K.P.Unnikrishnan, Vayalar Ravi, Avthan Singh and Hari Kishoredev were the leaders.

13 *The Statesman,* 3 May 1977.

14 T.A. Pai, C.Subramaniam and H.R.Gokale were the ministers.

15 *The Indian Express,* 11 December 1977.

16 They were Kamalapati Tripati, Marathagam Chandrasekhar, P.V. Narasimha Rao, A.P. Sharma,Virendra Varma, Syed Mir Quasim and Buta Singh.

17 *The Indian Express,* 3rd January 1978.

18 Rasheed Tabib, 'Should the Congress be one?' *The Illustrated Weekly of India,* 2-8 April 1978, p.17.

19 *The Hindu,* 3rd January 1978.

20 *Ibid.*

21 *The Indian Express,* 25th November 1978.

22 *Sunday;* 1 July 1979, p.15.

23 *The Indian Express,* 13 July 1979.

24 A.K. Antony in an interview to *Kerala Sabdam Weekly* 15 July 1979, p.11.

5

Promises and Performance: Failure and Disintegration of Janata Party

The Janata Party assumed power to the pledge of fulfilling the people's hopes and aspirations. The Janata manifesto was an ambitious draft for the solution of popular wishes and had the background of Jayaprakash Narayan's thought of *Total Revolution*. The *Total Revolution* of JP intended to transform the entire structure of Indian polity and reconstitute it in a novel way so that a welfare state would result at the end of the programme. But two years of Morarji raj destroyed all the hopes and converted "total revolution to a total failure."[1] Instead of showing coherent action and determined will power to act, the Janata regime showed that it was a bedlam, in which every pretended genius narrated his own pet schemes in a free-for-all affair. Any reviewer who looks back at the rise and fall of Janata government is reminded of the Chinese proverb 'it came like the roar of a tiger and disappeared like the tail of a snake'.

Promises and Performance

The schemes that the Janata party spoke to the people were innumerable[2] and the people expected something like a mini paradise coming into existence. But the Janata party's record of fulfilment of its political promises in its election manifesto of 1977 presents a mixed picture. In any Political System, two important tasks of a government are ensuring domestic tranquility and 'securing the blessings of liberty'.[3] Thus the Janata promised to restore the democratic features of an open competitive system as it functioned before the declaration of Emergency. But the Emergency was lifted by Mrs. Gandhi herself on 21ˢᵗ March 1977. During Emergency, the Supreme Court practically caved into the onrush of authoritarianism and refused to recognise even the citizen's right to life. The Janata government has given to the Judiciary its rightful place in our system of government. The outstanding example in this regard was the consultation of the Janata government with the Supreme Court on the question of setting up of special courts for trying persons guilty of illegal actions during the Emergency.

The setting up of various commissions of inquiry had been a part of the process of re-establishing the rule of law. One of the crucial questions before the country was to ensure that the provisions of the constitution do not once again become avenues for the imposition of personal rule or for the dictatorship of a single party. The Shah Commission had unravelled the working of our political institutions and our bureaucracy. One cannot provide any lasting remedy for the ailments of the body politic until we have a diagnosis. The commission had enabled us to do this.[4]

Although the Janata manifesto denounced the 42ⁿᵈ amendment to the constitution with great passion and gave its abolition high priority, it was here that the Janata government faltered. Oversensitive to the political situation and of the difficulties it faced in the Rajya Sabha, the Janata Party came in terms with the Congress opposition by retaining those clauses of that obnoxious act which seemed innocent. The Lok Sabha passed the 44ᵗʰ amendment on 3ʳᵈ August 1978, by seeking a consensus among divergent points of view. The bill ran into rough weather in the Raja Sabha which suggested several amendments. In the winter session of parliament in 1978, the Lok Sabha finally approved the 44ᵗʰ constitution amendment. The government has taken satisfaction in the fact that most, though not all of the clauses have been accepted. Dr. P.C. Chunder who moved the motion of the bill said that "half a loaf is better than none".[5] The amendment replaced the word 'armed rebellion' instead of 'internal disturbances' as a condition for the proclamation of internal Emergency. The amendment deleted clause (f) of Article

19 and Article 31 of the constitution dealing with right to property which was one of the fundamental rights. This fundamental right has been the bone of contention since the inception of the Constitution because of its inherent conflict with Part IV of the Constitution dealing with Directive Principles of State Policy. Since the Judiciary took the position that the Fundamental Rights are superior to the Directive Principles of State Policy, it became an object of attack in Parliament on the ground of being defender of privileged classes. Hence the amendment on fundamental rights and the right to property was made a statutory right under Article 300 and 301 (a). It also re-established some of the rights of the courts, taken away by the 42nd constitution amendment during the emergency.

Although the Janata party had fulfilled the core of its political charter, there remained items on its lists of unfulfilled promises. It dragged its feet in the abolition of the Maintenance of Internal Security Act, before finally repealing it. The manifesto also asserted that the Janata party would seek to widen the basis of participation through devolution and decentralisation. But the party opposed by cold shouldering the demand even for a discussion on centre-state relations. A real conflict of interest between the Centre and the States stemmed from the differing concepts of federalism in the National Development Council meeting in March 1978. While commenting on the observations made by Jyoti Basu, the Chief Minister of West Bengal[6] for more autonomy to the States, Prime Minister Morarji Desai said that there could not be any autonomy of the kind which would lead to the division of the country.[7] On the contrary, the dissolution of the State assemblies in 1977 by the Janata government was criticised by many as a severe blow to the autonomy of States and the nature of our "bargaining federalism."[8]

The report of the working group on autonomy for Akashvani and Doordarshan, which was appointed by Morarji government under the chairmanship of B.G. Varghese had suggested far reaching changes in their organizational structure and has recommended the setting up of a National Broadcasting Trust. However, the government had not taken any step to ensure the autonomy of the media.

The unification of education in the Indian federation was planned by P.C. Chundar, the Education Minister. He advised the 'ten plus two plus three pattern', which was given for a national debate. The planning was also reconstituted in its basic tenets and a new form called the Rolling Plan in the place of the five year plans was put into parliamentary discussion. According to the appraisal of the economy by the National Council of Applied Economic Research, the overall economic growth rate in 1978-79 was nearly three percent, much lower than the six percent in 1977-78.[9] Hence the change over to Janata regime indicated a worsening of the economy. In its election manifesto the Janata party accorded primacy to agriculture and rural reconstruction. It is true that following 1978 bumber harvest, prices of several agricultural commodities have been brought under control. At the same time the face of land reforms had not been satisfactory. The condition of Indian industry appeared to be in inverse proportion. The growth rate of over-all industrial production receded to 5.3 in 1977. The real reason behind this, seemed to be the haphazard industrial policy of the Janata government. Charan Singh in his "India's Economic Policy- the Gandhian Blueprint" (1978) condemned Nehru's policy of industrialisation, but at the sametime the government failed to develop small industries as an alternative, in spite of the incentives offered.

Morarji Desai on assuming power declared a time bound programme for the abolition of unemployment which reached about 10.2 million in 1st April 1977. But during the Janata regime the unemployment problem had worsened. The wider problem was that of under employment, which accounts for 20.6 million man-years, of which 75 per cent are in rural areas.[10] The Janata party's economic charter specifically envisaged the affirmation of the right to work. However, the central government rejected the demand for making this right into a fundamental right on the ground that such a step could be taken only when it is in a position to provide work for all people.

In the field of labour, the Janata government constituted a study group on wages, incomes and prices, under the chairmanship of S. Bhoothalingam. But the report of the study group was

44

opposed by all trade unions because of its anti-labour bias. The Industrial Relations Bill of 1978 also was opposed by the trade unions because of its undemocratic character, dominance of bureaucracy and unnecessary restrictions placed on trade unions. It was rightly called the "Black Bill"[11] for workers.

The prohibition policy of Morarji Desai faced stiff opposition and grounded to a halt. The submissive inflation re-started its onward course. The law and order situation deteriorated especially in the northern gangetic belt. As in the Congress rule, atrocities on Harijans were perpetrated. During the year ending 31st March 1978, 174 people belonging to the Scheduled castes were killed and 5,755 cases were registered in Uttar Pradesh. Corresponding figures for Madhya Pradesh were 63 and 3,798, and for Rajasthan 27 and 435.[12] Regarding the minorities, even the setting up of a Minorities Commission could not mitigate their problems. Instead, because of conflicts of views with those of the government the first Chairman of the Commission Minoo Masani resigned and the second Chairman M.R.A. Ansari threatened to resign.

Adding oil to the fire, the Akali-Nirankari conflict erupted in Delhi in November 1978, which caused the death of a score of people. The strike of para-military forces like Central Reserve Police Force (CRPF) and Central Industries Security Force (CISF) from May 1979 caused much damage to the law and order problem. The rift between Jammu region and Kashmir region resulted in violent clashes in the Kashmir valley. The agrarian revolt spread much in Tamil Nadu districts of Coimbatore and Tanchavur. All this gave the impression of a nonfunctioning government and remembered the words of April Carter that 'All attempts to create a revolutionary authority are necessarily examples of false authority.[13]

The discussions within the Janata Party, political rivalries, personality conflicts and the habit of airing differences in the open have combined to weaken the effectiveness of the Janata government. So let us turn to the group rivalries which took place within the Janata party and worked as a catalystic agent to its breaking away and ultimately led to the re-emergence of Indira Gandhi and the Congress (I).

Disintegration of Janata Party

History made the spring of 1977 when five parties came together to fight the ruling Congress in the March elections. They vowed to remain united if they came to power at the centre under the banner of the Janata party. But for all its professions of unity, it crumbled down due to many reasons. The most important of which was that, the party failed to organise itself as an ideologically and functionally cohesive unit and to go anywhere near implementing the programme of the JP movement. It functioned as if it was an alliance of constituent parties; it forgot the ideology of *Total Revolution* and hopelessly got itself trapped in an activity of self-preservation for the sake of remaining in power. In other words the Janata party's tragedy was that, being a combination of opposite elements - those who stood for traditional values and status quo and those who professed basic changes in society-it lacked the ethos of either.[14] As a result the political field was turbulent with internal splits and divisions in the Janata parliamentary parties at the centre and in various states. The Central Parliamentary Party was bipolarised with a weak middle. The actual five constituents merged, divided unevenly into two camps, one supporting the Jana Sangh hard core, acting as the organisational base and the other the rural farmer lobby- the backward caste colour-led by Charan Singh. The balance was kept in the middle by the old Congressmen and the 'young turks' under the party president S. Chandrasekhar.

In the States the Chief Ministers were repeatedly asked to seek fresh mandate from the State parliamentary parties. Shantakumar in Himachal Pradesh and Nilamani Rout Rai in Orissa survived the destablisation moves. In Uttar Pradesh, the home base of Charan Singh, Ram Naresh Yadav was toppled. But with the help of H.N. Bahuguna, Charan Singh succeeded in installing Banarasi Das in the place of Ram Naresh Yadav on 27th February 1979. In Bihar the toppling game took the colour of a struggle between backward and forward classes for existence. Fearing the strength of the backward classes, the Scheduled Castes and Scheduled Tribes sided with the forward classes and tilted the balance. Consequently Karpoori Thakur, the socialist leader of Bihar politics was toppled on 19th April and Ram Sundar Das was installed as Chief Minister on 21st April 1979.

In Haryana which some called the Jat land, Devilal survived one no-confidence motion but another was forced on him and he resigned on 23rd June 1979. Bhajan Lal was installed in his place on 28th of the same month. Thus, he was of nerves in the Janata party left no victors but only losers. It is clear from the above circumstances that the necessary consensus on the procedural principles among the Janata leadership was lacking.

The crisis that erupted in the Janata party in the middle of 1978 and led to its split was due to a clash of personalities, especially between Morarji Desai and Charan Singh. Morarji Desai wanted to retain his position and Charan Singh was in a greater hurry to become the Prime Minister. The issues relating to the contentious situation where Kanthi Desai issue, on which Prime Minister Morarji Desai rejected the plea of Charan Singh. Charan Singh requested that the government may institute an inquiry into the manner in which Kanthi Desai, the Prime Minister's son, had amassed wealth. On the economic front Charan Singh accused Morarji Desai as anti-agriculturist, anti-artisan and anti-people.[15] Further, there occurred a difference between them on the swiftness and mode of trial of Indira Gandhi.

The result of all these was that the Prime Minister Morarji Desai quite consistently demanded resignations of both Charan Singh and Raj Narain from the Cabinet. They readily complied with the request and four other ministers followed them. Devi Lal described the Prime Minister's action as part of a conspiracy against Charan Singh and Raj Narain by those at the helm of affairs of the government and the Janata Party.[16] For a few months this stale-mate continued. At this juncture the valient efforts of A.B. Vajpayee and some others lessened the stiff stand of Morarji Desai and Charan Singh was reinducted with the additional post of Deputy Prime Ministership. The fact was that the first action against Charan Singh was possible only because of the stable support of the Jana Sangh and the second was possible only because the Jana Sangh insisted on attaining peace. The Jana Sangh factor was important because intra-party democracy was not established in Janata and there was no election since its inception. This was mainly due to the fear of the other constituents that the Jana Sangh may overpower them by sheer weight of numbers. So the party remained a 'compromise party'.[17]

After the resolution of the crisis Charan Singh organised a Kisan rally in Delhi. He also consolidated his position among the farmers by allocating a lumpsum agricultural subsidy of Rs. 450 crores in the budget of 1979. The seventy one lakhs fund given to him by his supporters, added much strength to his position and then the question was choosing the propitious moment. On the ideological plane Charan Singh succeeded in winning the support of the Socialists, a golden opportunity to rally round the anti-RSS forces. He immediately went for a rest in Suraj kund, which was actually a plotting in solitude for the overthrow of Morarji government.

Adding strength to Charan Singh, the controversy of dual membership of RSS and Jana Sangh was however never resolved. Along with the socialists he argued against the contention of the RSS being a social, cultural and religious organization. Thus the Janata Party was getting divided into two rival groups one led by the Jana Sangh and the Congress (O) and the other by the BLD - Socialist combine. The CFD group seemed to be taking position statewise. The fact that the Jana Sangh would not disown the RSS was demonstrably made clear on 4th March 1979, at Delhi, at the RSS rally which was attended by cabinet ministers. It was a reply to the 'Kisan Sammelan' of the B L D. The Socialists were to be left behind. Thus, Industries Minister George Fernandes proposed to convene shortly a meeting of the Socialists to discuss the implementation of the policies and programmes of the Janata party contained in its election manifesto.

At last the Parliament was summoned in the middle of 1979. Just to project the inefficiency of the Prime Minister Morarji Desai, the opposition leader Y.B. Chavan introduced a no-confidence motion in the Lok Sabha. The resignations from the Janata Parliamentary Party were started with Raj Narain and ten of his associates, who formed the Janata(S). The next section of twelve was mostly Muslim MPs forced to resign because the main trump card of Raj Narain was the question of RSS. On 14th July, George Fernandes, Purushotham Lal Kaushik and Bhanu Pratap Singh resigned from the Morarji Cabinet. The flood of exit started and speedily the other members followed suit and numbered about hundred within a week. The final curtain came down when Charan Singh also defected and Morarji Desai submitted his resignation on 15th July 1979.

In this political imbroglio Indira Gandhi played a brilliant card by supporting Charan Singh for an alternative ministry. Charan Singh went for the bait and became Prime Minister on 28th July 1979. But within a short period Congress (I) withdrew the support to Charan Singh Ministry and he resigned on 20th August, without facing the parliament and advised the president for mid-term poll.[18] The President dissolved the parliament on 22nd August 1979 and asked the people to have a self evaluation and confirmed decision about their future leaders.[19] Thus came the Lok Sabha elections of January 1980. The election witnessed the electoral debacle of the disintegrated and demoralised Janata Party and its splinter groups.[20] Within two and a half years, the edifice that was painfully constructed by the people laid in ruins and appeared beyond repair.

Writing on the crisis followed by the resignation of Charan Singh as Prime Minister, Devaraj Urs said, "India is facing today a crisis of great magnitude, fundamentally this is a crisis of character."[21] The veteran parliamentarian Prof. Madhu Dandavate, said that the change of government from Morarji Desai to Charan Singh had been the product of a crisis precipitated basically by power politics at the summit.[22] In the opinion of S. Chandrasekhar, the president of the Janata Party, "the problem is not of ideological drift but of moral erosion and complete collapse of ethical values that democratic society must preserve".[23] None of these explanations are comprehensive. In fact, the formation of the Janata party was not an organic growth. The constituent units came together to survive the oppressive Emergency. No constituent of the party was really prepared to go beyond a united front or a federal party. The experience of the twenty-seven months had shown that without a common tradition, a common political culture, genuine commitment to programmes and above all self-abnegation, such experiments are not likely to succeed.

Thus, the causes of Janata downfall were variously ascribed to the egoistic and centralist tendencies of its leaders, factional struggle among parties constituting the Janata Party, inefficiency of the Janata raj etc. Overall it gives the scenario of a Shakespearian tragedy with heroes of great ability crumbling down due to a single tragic flaw. However, the conclusion is inescapable that the main catalystic agent, which led to the disintegration of the Janata party was the RSS with its *"Hindu Rashtra"* slogan. The lack lustre performance of Morarji Desai and his friends and the petty ambitions of Charan Singh and his associates are some of the other causes. The mandate of 1980 mid-term poll is loud and clear, the eclipse of the official Congress and the rise of Indira Gandhi as the representative of Congress legacy, underline the importance of personality in Indian politics. The euphoria of the March 1977 election became a thing of the past, a memory to be recorded by the chronicler and commented on by the historians of the future.

Notes and References:

1   J.A. Naik, *From Total Revolution to Total Failure*, New Delhi, 1979, p.111.

2   See Appendix I

3   Robert K. Carr, Marver H, Bernstein and Walter F. Murphy, *American Democracy in Theory and Practice*, New York, 1975 p. 23.

4   A.P. Aiyar, *'Two Years of Janata'* *The Illustrated Weekly of India*, 18-24 March 1979, p. 9.

5   Olga Tellis, 'Janata Deserves a Better Image' *Sunday*, 30 December 1979, p.17.

6   See Appendix - 3.

7   *The Hindu;* 24 January, 1978.

8   For an analysis of 'bargaining federalism' see W.H. Morris Jones, *The Government and Politics of India,* New Delhi, 1971, p.143.

9   Shiv Lal, 'Party Politics in India: Janata's Fiasco of Promises and Performance', *The Election Archives,* New Delhi, 1979, p.7.

10   S.D. Punekar and Brahm Prakash, 'Promise and Performance', *The Illustrated Weekly of India,* 18-24 March 1979, p.12.

11   V.N. Tewari; *12 Willingdon Crescent: Indian Politics at the Crossroads,* Delhi, 1979 p. 84.

12   S.D Punekar and Brahm Prakash, *Promise and Performance,* pp. 12-13.

13   April Carter, *Authority and Democracy,* London, 1979, p.87.

14   Sachidanand Sinha, *The Permanent Crisis in India: After Janata What?,* p. 132.

15   *The Times of India,* 12 July 1978.

16   *Ibid.,* 1 July 1978.

17   V.N. Tewari, *12 Willingdon Crescent: Indian Politics at the Crossroads,* p. 79.

18   *The Indian Express,* 21 August 1979.

19   *The Hindu,* 23 August 1979.

20   For details see, Appendix-2.

21   Devaraj Urs, 'Pragmatism is the Only Answer to India's Problems', *The Indian Express,*17 August 1979.

22   Madhu Dandavate, 'Crisis Rooted in Summit Power Politics', *The Indian Express,* 11 August 1979.

23   S. Chandrasekhar, 'Betrayal of Janata Party', *The Indian Express* 16, August 1979.

6

Coalition At The Centre National Front Forms The Government

The ninth Lok Sabha election of November 1989 has been described as a watershed in Indian politics. For the second time since independence, the Congress party[1] has been ousted from power and a minority National Front government formed with the help of the Bharatiya Janata Party and the Left Front. The election became a major occasion for the expression of the people's feelings, but the electorate has given no clear verdict to any party. The voters rejected the Congress (I) and its leader and Prime Minister Rajiv Gandhi at the national level, while expressing a surprisingly different response to the non-Congress (I) governments in the South. How did this happen? The question leads us to the pre-election scenario of the Rajiv Gandhi dispensation and the endeavours of the fragmented opposition to come together under a common political umbrella-the Janata Dal - and then under a broad-based national platform-the National Front, against the misdeeds and authoritarianism of the Congress (I).

The failure and disintegration of the Janata experiment of 1977-79, led to the seventh Lok Sabha election of January 1980. As expected the Congress (I) led by Indira Gandhi came out successful and thus marked the return of the single-party-dominant system in India. The election proved the total disintegration of the Janata Party.[1] In the eighth Lok Sabha election of December 1984, the Congress (I) thrived on the wave unleashed by the national tragedy-the assassination of Indira Gandhi. The sympathy wave swept the polls and the Congress (I), under the new Prime Minister Rajiv

Gandhi shattered all previous records by capturing a three-fourths majority in the House.[2] The earlier record set by the Congress in the second general election of 1957, under the towering stewardship of Jawaharlal Nehru was broken on the threshold of martyrdom. However, the Congress (I) suffered in Andhra Pradesh at the hands of Telugu Desam of N.T. Rama Rao. The Telugu Desam won 30 out of the 42 seats, and became the first regional party to become the largest opposition party in the Lok Sabha.

The Janata Party secured only 10 seats and the re-organised Bharatiya Janata Party-former Jana Sangh-only two seats. The Left parties managed to secure 33 seats. So powerful was the wave that the national leaders of the opposition parties like Atal Behari Vajpayee (President of the BJP), S. Chandrasekhar (President of the Janata party), and H.N. Bahuguna (Vice-President of the DMKP) were defeated.

Emergence of Janata Dal and National Front

The lessons of the parliamentary elections of 1980 and 1984, turned the attention of the fragmented opposition to the sixth Lok Sabha election of 1977. However, it was only after the upheavals in the ruling Congress (I) and the emergence of Viswanath Pratap Singh as the leader of the Jan Morcha[3] and his transformation into a charismatic mass leader, that the idea of a united opposition came back to life. At that time, the political atmosphere was more vitiated by violence and criminalisation of politics and public life, corruption in high places, abuse of authority and trust, the re-emergent authoritarianism and the arrogance of the ruling party and its leader Rajiv Gandhi.

The unity efforts among opposition parties were always marred by personal ambitions of several leaders. Later when fresh attempts were made, controversies over Ajith Singh's induction as Janata Party President, Chandrasekhar's opposition to merger and Ram Dhan's resolve to stay away from the formation of a new party and preserve the Jana Morcha identity came to the forefront. But after many futile attempts and behind the door confabulations a centrist grouping called the Samajwadi Janata Dal was formed on 26th July 1988 at Bangalore, in a meeting participated by the leaders of the Jan Morcha, Lok Dal, Janata and the Congress (S). The meeting declared V.P. Singh as the new party's President, Ajith Singh as Secretary-General and Devilal as the Chairman of the Parliamentary Board.[4]

The desire of the ranks of all parties and the opposition-minded voters was so strong that ultimately leaders with a modicum of realism had to bow before this sentiment and the centrist opposition combine - the Janata, the Lok Dal and the Jana Mocha - became a united single party - the Janata Dal, on 11th October 1988 at Bangalore.[5] The meeting unanimously selected V.P. Singh as the founding president of the Janata Dal.[6] The Congress (S) which had been a party in the formation of the Samajwadi Janata Dal kept out of the proceedings due to some technical objections regarding the modalities adopted and the nature of the constitution of the new party.[7]

Calling for an urgent re-orientation of national priorities and resource allocation the Janata Dal declared that, planning should be centered around human labour as the key asset and the right to work to all citizens as the basic imperative. The Party guaranteed action on the recommendations of the Mandal Commission Report, to better the lot of other backward classes. It also emphasised the need for effective and genuine decentralisation of economic and political power.[8] Commenting on the formation of the Janata Dal, S. Chandrasekhar, former president of the Janata Party, said that "the mending of broken hearts and propping up human dignity and self-respect is the essence of the policy of the new party".[9] While the formation of the new centrist party was welcomed by the two Communist parties, the BJP President, L.K. Advani denounced the centrist groups as a squabbling lot.[10]

Meanwhile, efforts were made to form a National Front of the centrist and some of the regional political parties. Consequently, on 27th May 1988, the leaders of ten opposition parties[11] met at Vijayawada and resolved on direct contest against the Congress (I) in the Lok Sabha and State legislative assembly elections. As a final step, on 7th August of the same year, the National Front officially came in to being at a meeting held in Andhra Pradesh Bhavan at New Delhi.[12] The meeting unanimously appointed V.P.Singh as the convenor and N.T. Rama Rao as the chairman of the National Front. A Presidium cum Central Committee of eleven members[13] was also constituted. Thus after a decade of the Janata experiment of 1977-79, the opposition once again joined together to fight against the misdeeds and authoritarianism of the Congress (I).

Electoral Alliances

The term of the eighth Lok Sabha was to expire in January 1990, but before the expiry of its term on 17th October 1989 the Election Commission announced the elections of the 9th Lok Sabha will be held between November 22 and 26, 1989. Generally, the non-Congress (I) parties were divided into three groups, that is the National Front, the Left Front and the BJP-Shiv Sena combination. So far as the Left Front, and the National Front were concerned, they had a complete electoral understanding, except on Bihar, where CPI had an alliance with Jharkhand Mukti Morcha and therefore contested some seats against Janata Dal. In Tamil Nadu and Andhra Pradesh, there was a complete understanding among all the national parties and as a result there was one to one contest in these two states.

The most important alliance in the Hindi belt was between Janata Dal and BJP which differed from state to state. There was a complete adjustment of seats between these two parties in Haryana, Gujarat and Rajasthan. There was partial alliance between Janata Dal and BJP in Delhi, Bihar, Madhya Pradesh and Uttar Pradesh. There was no alliance between these two parties in Himachal Pradesh, Jammu & Kashmir, Orissa, Karnataka, Maharashtra and Chandigarh. In the Communist strongholds BJP contested against the Left Front and in Maharashtra the BJP had an alliance with the fanatical Shiv Sena and ensured triangular contests against National Front- Left alliance on one side and the Congress (I) on the other. In Kerala the BJP indirectly supported the Congress (I), in order to defeat the ruling Left Democratic Front.

So far as the Congress (I) was concerned, it had alliances with the National Conference in Jammu & Kashmir, with AIADMK and United Communist Party of India (UCPI) in Tamil Nadu and in Kerala with the communal parties like the Indian Union Muslim League, Kerala Congress (M) and casteist parties such as Socialist Republican Party (of Ezhavas) and National Democratic Party (of Nairs). In Andhra, there was an indirect understanding between the Congress (I) and Majlis-e-Itehad e-Muslimeen. In addition, the Congress (I) did not put any candidate against the Gorkha National Liberation Front in West Bengal.

In spite of the fact that the non-Congress (I) parties such as the Janata Dal and the BJP tried to have an alliance in the Hindi belt, they had an understanding only on 265 seats and in about 50 constituencies they had friendly contests. Besides this, the BJP contested all the 20 seats in Kerala and 19 in West Bengal. There were a large number of independents in the fray. Only one candidate returned unopposed-a National Conference candidate from Kashmir.

Performance of Political Parties[14]

After the 1977 Lok Sabha election it was thought that the process of institutionalisation of two-party system had started in India. But an analysis of the 1989 poll results does not indicate any such clear trend regarding the emerging pattern of the party system. One of the important peculiarities of the ninth Lok Sabha is that, for the first time since independence none of the political parties has got an absolute majority and a hung Lok Sabha has been returned.

Table 6. 1

1989 Lok Sabha Election: Party Position (State wise)

Sl. No.	State/Union Territories	No.of Seats	Con-gress (I)	Janata Dal	BJP	CPI	CPI (M)	Others/Inde-pendents
1	2	3	4	5	6	7	8	**9**
1.	Andhra Pradesh	42	39					Telugu Desam-2 Majilis-e-Musilmeen-1
2	Arunachal Pradesh	2	2					Jharkhand Mukthi
3	Bihar	54	4	31	9	4	1	Morcha-3, Marxist Co-ordination-1, M.G.P -1
4	Goa	2	1					
5	Gujarat	26	3	11	12			
6	Haryana	10	4	6				
7	Himachal Pradesh	4	1		3			National Conference-3, Ind-1
8	Jammu & Kashmir	6	2					
9	Karnataka	28	27	1			2	Congress
10	Kerala	20	14					(S)-1, IUL-2,
11	Madhya Pradesh	40	8	4	27			Kerala-Con-gress (M) - 1, Independent
12	Maharash-tra	48	28	5	12	1		-1, Shiv Sena -2
13	Manipur	2	2					
14	Meghalaya	2	2					
15	Mizoram	1	1					
16	Nagaland	1	1					
17	Orissa	21	3	16		1	1	

Sl. No.	State/Union Territories	No.of Seats	Con-gress (I)	Janata Dal	BJP	CPI	CPI (M)	Others/Independents
1	2	3	4	5	6	7	8	9
18	Punjab	13	2	1				Akali Dal (Mann) -6, (BSP-1, Ind-3
19	Rajasthan	25		11	13		1	
20	Sikkim	1						
21	Tamilnadu	39	25			1		Sikkim Sangram Parrishad-1, AIADMK-11, UCPI-1, Muslim League (S)1
22	Tripura	2	2					
23	West Bengal	42	4			3	27	RSP-4, Forward Bloc-3., GNLF-1
24	Uthar Pradesh	85	15	54	8	2	1	BSP-2, Hindu Mahasaha-1, Ind-2
25	Andamans Nicobar	1	1					
26	Chandigarh	1		1				
27	Dadra & Nagar Haveli	1						Independent-1, Independent-1
28	Daman & Dieu	1						
29	Delhi	7	2	1	4			
30	Lakshadweep	1	1					
31	Pondicherry	1	1					
	Total	529	195	142	88	12	33	59

Elections were not held in Assam-(13) seats.

The election result gave a severe jolt to the Congress (I). Out of 529 seats for which elections were held, the Congress (I) won only 195 seats and its allies and supporters 17 seats.[15] On the other side the Janata Dal won 143 seats, the Left Front 52 seats and the BJP 88 seats. It is important to see that the BJP winning an estimated 15 per cent of the popular vote with a steady rise over the years from 3 percent in the first post-independence election in 1952. Thus the electoral verdict hinted at the nation's most untractables. In a sense the polls exonerated the BJP's espousal of 'Hindutva' and stoking the embers of majority communalism.[16]

Prime Minister Rajiv Gandhi was the single most important and overarching issue at the hustings and the verdict was clearly against him. However, the south showed a different trend revealing the National Front's area of weakness. V.P. Singh and the other Janata Dal leaders had not come down to south for campaign. The southern electrorate was just as disenchanted with their state governments - TDP in Andhra, DMK in Tamil Nadu and Janata in Karnataka. Even the Left Democratic Front in Kerala fumbled. Consequently, the Congress (I) swept up almost all the parliamentary seats in the four southern states as in 1977. Besides the southern states, in Maharashtra also the Congress (I) performance was better due to the triangular contests ensured by the Shiva Sena - BJP alliance. There were as many as sixteen political parties that did not have any representation in the eighth Lok Sabha and were able to win seats in the ninth Lok Sabha with a tally of 35 seats. The performance of independents was a little better as compared to 1984. They were able to win eleven seats as compared to five in 1984. The representation of women decreased from 42 in 1984 to 27 in 1989.[17]

Table 6.2

Performance of Political Parties in 1989 Lok Sabha Election

Sl. No.	Name of Political party	Seats con-tested in 1989	*Seats won in 1989	*Seats won in 1984	Loss/ Gain
1	2	3	4	5	6
1	Indian National Congress (I)	529	195	403	- 208
2	Janata Dal	237	142	Nil	+ 142
3	Bharatiya Janata Party	228	88	2	+ 86
4	Communist Party of India	51	12	6	+ 6
5	Communist Party of India (Maxist)	65	33	22	+ 11
6	AIADMK	11	11	7	+ 4
7	Akali Dal (Mann)	8	6	Nil	+ 6
8	Revolutionary Socialist Party	5	4	Nil	+ 4
9	All India Forward Bloc	3	3	Nil	+ 3
10	Bahujan Samaj Party (BSP)	179	3	Nil	+ 3
11	Jharkand Mukthi Morcha	14	3	Nil	+ 3
12	National Conference	3	3	3	Nil
13	Telugu Desam Party	33	2	30	-28
14	Indian Union Muslim League	2	2	2	Nil
15	Kerala Congress (M)	1	1	1	Nil
16	Indian People's Front	2	1	Nil	+1
17	Assam Gana Sangram Parishad	-	-	7	- -

Sl. No.	Name of Political party	Seats con- tested in 1989	*Seats won in 1989	*Seats won in 1984	Loss/ Gain
1	2	3	4	5	6
18	Indian Socialist Congress (S)	8	1	7+4a	- 3
19	Indian Union Muslim League (S)	2	1	Nil	+ 1
20	Sikkim Sangram Parishad	1	1	Nil	+ 1
21	United Communist Party of India (T.N)	2	1	Nil	+ 1
22	Marxist Co-ordination Committee	1	1	Nil	+ 1
23	Majlis Itehad-e-eMusilmeen	1	1	Nil	+ 1
24	Maharashtrawadi Gomathak Party	1	1	Nil	+ 1
25	Hindu Maha Sabha	1	1	Nil	+ 1
26	Shiv Sena	16	2	Nil	+ 2
27	Janata Party	17	Nil	10	- 10
28	Dravida Munneetta Kazhagam	30	Nil	1	- 1
29	Others	636	Nil	14	- 14
30	Independents	4006	10	5	+ 5
	Total	6039	521	522	X

* In 1989, Elections were not held in Assam (13 seats).

* Elections took place in Assam and Punjab in 1985.

(a) In 1985 the Congress(s) won 4 seats in Assam.

One of the most important disturbing developments which has taken place in the elections was the criminalisation of the political process in the country. Now there is an increasing nexus between the politicians and the criminals of the underworld and the use of the muscle power is on the increase. At present, the criminals instead of helping the politicians, have started entering into political arena themselves and for winning the elections, they use strong arm tactics with the support of the party politicians. The use of hoodlums, bandits and criminals in this election was on a very large scale and in many constituencies, including Amethi, from where Prime Minister Rajiv Gandhi contested the election. Because of rigging and booth-capturing the Election Commission had to order repoll in as many as 1,670 booths. Moreover, several persons were killed in poll violence.

Why did the Congress (I) Lost?

The National Front's biggest political advantage was its achievement after months of parleys of having ensured one to one contests for most seats in the Hindi belt. Thus, as in 1977 the foremost factor which contributed to the defeat of the Congress (I) was the opposition unity. The National Front forged an electoral alliance with the other two opposition groups - the BJP and the Left Front. However, there was no electoral understanding between the Leftists and the BJP. The Communists and the BJP disliked each other intensely. Consequently, the National Front groped towards an elaborate strategy whereby the Left Front and the BJP independently arrived at a direct understanding with the Janata Dal.

Interestingly, the strategic responses of the National Front and the Congress (I) to the explosive event at Ayodhya had indeed proved to be the turning point in the fortunes of both. Just as the Congress (I) High Command miscalculated the Babri Masjid-Ram Janma Bhoomi controversy and failed to see that at a critical point its already deteriorating prospects were well and truly lost, exposing the party as possessing no real political faith and in fact anchored to a strategy of opportunism. The Janata Dal and its leader V.P. Singh had in an intuitive move, grasped the significance of alienation of Muslims over the Ayodhya event and struck the right political chord. V.P. Singh even refused to address public meetings jointly with the BJP, while the Congress (I) caved into the pressure of the increasingly shrill Hindu communalist sentiment.[18] Under the Congress regime in Delhi and Uttar Pradesh, the cordons were lifted in Ayodhya and a mass of Hindu communalist activists rushed in to perform the foundation laying ceremony for a Ram temple as an outraged Muslim community watched horror-struck at the sudden dropping of pretenses by a supposedly secular party. The preceding communal riots exposed Congress (I) pretension on the defence of secularism and minority interests. At the same time, the party was not even to enjoy the advantage of Hindu vote, which was taken away by the BJP. Earlier, the carnage of Sikhs which followed Indira Gandhi's assassination in 1984 showed the extent to which communal politics of the government in power are destablishing the nation when the entire fabric of Indian society was torn asunder during just one weekend.[19]

Another miscalculation of the Congress (I) was its reliance on the two populist oriented programmes - the Panchayati Raj and Nagarpalika legislations[20] along with the Jawahar Rozgar Yojna. The continual harping on the two new programmes and the virtual silence on the highly effective litany of charges levelled against the party and its leaders. The opposition parties did articulate a common stance, shared concern and outrage at the systematic and deliberate erosion of public institutions, a passionate condemnation of corruption and venality in high places and a determination to oust the Congress (I) from power.

The opposition kept on Bofors gun and H D W submarine issues alive. The Bofors pay-off scandal which had been haunting Congress (I) government for more than two years acquired new dimensions following the fresh disclosure about the contents of the diary of Martin Ardbo, the chairman of Swedish armament manufacturing company which also raised accusing finger at Rajiv Gandhi.[21] Thus a few months before the announcement of the elections 105 members of the Lok Sabha belonging to all the major opposition parties resigned from the Lok Sabha on this issue. In this defence deal a commission of more than sixty crores of rupees was taken and the opposition alleged that the Prime Minister Rajiv Gandhi was involved in it. Along with it the report of the Comptroller and Auditor General also damaged the credibility of Rajiv Gandhi and his government.

While criticising the economic policies of the Congress (I) the National Front assured the people the strengthening of the nation's unity, integrity and security; amendment of the constitution for making right to work as a fundamental right; implementation of constitutional safeguards assured to weaker sections like scheduled castes, scheduled tribes, backward classes; women and minorities and providing employment and educational opportunities to socially deprived sections with the terms of reference of the Mandal Commission, remunerative prices to Kisans and effective implementation of minimum wages to agricultural labour; eradication of corruption; implementation of the inter-state council etc.[22] The opposition alleged that the compromises made by Rajiv Gandhi have seriously weakened national unity and integrity while appeasement of various communal forces has likewise diluted the commitment to secularism.[23]

In addition to the causes mentioned above there were other causes of the defeat also, such as increasing unemployment, rising prices, political instability in Congress (I) ruled states because of frequent changes of the Chief Ministers. The amendment of the Commission of Inquiry Act which permitted the Union government not to place the report of the inquiry commissions before Parliament was also not liked by the public because by using this amended Act, the Thakkar Commission Report of Indira Gandhi's assassination was neither shown to the President nor was it placed before the Parliament.[24] The amendment of Postal Bill, and the controversial 59th Constitution Amendment (1988)[25] also had a negative effect on the image of Rajiv Gandhi and the Congress (I). All these factors were responsible for the defeat of Congress (I) in the 9th Lok Sabha elections of 1989.

National Front Forms the Government

With an uncertain line up with no party in absolute majority attention had been drawn to the critical role of President R. Venkataraman. But the situation simplified itself when the Congress (I) chose not to try to stay in office. This was no renunciatory juncture for even if installed in power the Congress (I) would have been voted out in the very first trial of strength in the Lok Sabha because the numbers were against it. It was a change for the second time in four decades and Viswanath Pratap Singh sworn in as the Prime Minister of India on 2nd December 1989, after his election as the leader of the Janata Dal, and also of the National Front, and the assurances of support to him by the BJP and the Left Front.[26]

The BJP President L.K. Advani spelt out his party's support to the National Front government in a letter to the National Front leaders in reply to their communication seeking support.[27] The CPI and the CPI (M) too made clear their ideas either in their notes to the National Front or through public statements. The CPI General Secretary, C. Rajeswara Rao stressed that their support to the National Front was based on "secular and democratic policies", and on the condition that the new government was not to include communal parties like the BJP, Muslim League etc.[28] The CPI(M) also offered its unconditional support to the V.P. Singh government.[29] Thus the National Front had formed a government in Delhi but sustaining of the Janata Dal's popular vote faced heavy odds from the beginning with the need to balance its two supporters outside-the BJP and the Left Front- two polar opposites, and the need to meet enhanced popular expectations and the sensitive Babri-Masjid- Ram Janmabhoomi controversy.[30]

Notes and References:

1   In 1977 it was the Indian National Congress and in 1989, the Congress (I).

2   See Appendix-2.

3   See *Ibid.*

65

4   The Jan Morcha was the new political formation emerged out of the upheavals in the Congress (I) and was led by V.P. Singh, Arun Nehru, Arif Mohammad Khan, Satyapal Mallik and Ram Dhan.

5   *The Indian Express*, 27 July, 1988.

6   *The Hindu*, 12 October, 1988.

7   The Bangalore meeting also unanimously endorsed 'haldar within a wheel' as Janata Dal's election symbol and a flag, a green one on which the party's election symbol be re-imposed in white colour.

8   *The Hindu*, 12 October, 1988.

9   See Appendix-4.

10   J.C. Johari, *Indian Government and Politics*, Delhi, 1989, p. 965.

11   Madhu Limaye, 'The State of the Opposition' *The Hindu*, 2 December, 1988.

12   The ten opposition parties were - Janata Party, Lok Dal, BJP, Jan Morcha, Telugu Desam, Assam Gana Sangram Parishad, Manipur People's Party, Panthers Party of J & K, and the Socialist Unity Centre of India.

13   *The Hindu*, 8 August, 1988.

14   The Presidium of the National Front consisted of   V.P. Singh, N.T. Rama Rao (President TDP), Ajith Singh (President, Janata), H.N, Bahuguna (President, Lok Dal), Sarathchandra Sinha (President, Congress (S), Ram Dhan (Convenor, Jan Morcha), P.K. Mahantha (President, AGP), M. Karunanidhi (President, DMK), Devilal, Ramakrishna Hedge and Biju Patnaik.

15   For a Comparative analysis of the Lok Sabha election results since 1952 to 1989, See Appendix-2.

16   The Congress (I)'s allies were the AIADMK-11, the National Conference-3, the IUML_2 and the Kerala Congress (M)-1.

17   B. Ramesh Babu, 'Opportunity for the Opposition', *Seminar*, No.368, April 1990, p.22.

18   For details see, J.R. Siwach, *Dynamics of Indian Government and Politics*, New Delhi, 1990, pp.851-852.

19   Malini Parthasarathy, 'The Winning Strategy' *Front Line*, No.25, December 9-22, 1989, p.12.

20   The Constitution 73rd and 74th Amendments.

21 Rajai Koathari, 'Grassroot Movements: The Search for Alternatives', *The Illustrated Weekly of India,* April 29, 1984, p.24.

22 *The Indian Express,* 5 November, 1989.

23 See for details the Election Manifestoes of the Janata Dal and the National Front (1989).

24 *The Times of India,* 15 November, 1989.

25 J.R.Siwach, *Ibid.* p.858.

26 The 59th Constitution Amendment (Articles-352, 356, 358, 359-Article 359-A inserted) restored the declaration of emergency in Punjab or any part thereof in the name of 'internal disturbances' and President's power to suspend enforcement of Fundamental Rights during Emergency for a period of two years.

27 *The Hindu,* 3 December 1989.

28 See Appendix - 5.

29 K.K. Katyal, 'Triumph and Trial', *Frontline,* December 9- 22, 1989, P, 10-11.

30 *The Hindu,* 3 December, 1989.

7

The Communal Dimension: Politics at Cross Roads

The 1989 Lok Sabha elections ended the era of decisive majorities, of single-party hegemony for the time being. It ushered a new phase of coalition politics, the like which the country had not tried so far at the national level. The electorate acted administering heavy blows to the ruling elite. But the new dispensation - the National Front government backed by the BJP and the Left Front-had instability built into it[1] because of the nature of the coalition itself. What bound the Janata Dal/National Front and their supporters was the realisation that the electorate unequivocally rejected the Congress (I) and that they would be undermining the verdict by adopting a course that paves the way for its return to power. Because of their mutual allergies, the outside supporters were not prepared to join the government and if one were to share office the other would withdraw support. At last the inevitable happened on 23rd October 1990, when the BJP withdrew its support to the National Front government as a reaction against the arrest of L.K. Advani on his 'rath yatra' towards Ayodhya, on the Mandir-Masjid issue. But as everybody knew, the seeds of the crisis were firmly sworn in the decision of the National Front government to implement the recommendations of the Mandal Commission.

The Second Backward Classes Commission with Bindeshwari Prasad Mandal as Chairman was appointed by the Morarji Desai government on 20 December 1978 and submitted its Report on 31 December 1980. The Janata Dal had promised the implementation of the recommendations and this had figured as the 36th item in the party's manifesto. The report held out prospects for the entry of a host of socially disadvantaged backward castes into secure government employment. V. P. Singh had assumed that the caste system also embodied political power. To break the stranglehold on political power it was necessary to strengthen the hands of lower castes under the rubric of "other backward castes" or OBCs.[2] It was however in the inevitable logic of the support extended by a right-wing party to a centrist secular one to form the government, that a headlong clash took place which finally led to the collapse of V. P. Singh government. Before looking into that let us have a look into the overall performance of the V.P. Singh government and the causes of its downfall.

Little Time for Performance

Eleven months is a short period to assess the performance of a national government which survived from one crisis to another. Yet, among the distinctive characteristics of the National Front government, apart from the commitment to "openness and values in public life", the rural orientation represented by the decision to increase the share of investment in the rural sector upto 49 percent of the budgetory allocation of 1990-91 and to write off farm loans below Rs. 10,000. The decision of the government to give autonomy for Doordarshan and All India Radio, a follow up to the Prasar Bharati Bill of the erstwhile Janata government, with its imperfections, represents at least a theoretical break from the centralized and controlled regime of Congress government. The government also decided to appoint a Judicial Commission to ensure the independence of Judiciary.[3]

The National Front government gave extension of reservation for Scheduled Castes and Scheduled Tribes giving statutory status to the SC-ST Commission. Constitution 62nd amendment to this effect was made in December 1989. Added to this, Dr. B.R.Ambedkar, Chairman of the Drafting Committee of the Constitution of India, was given due respect and honour by unveiling his photo in his birth centenary year. Further during the period, the National Development Council had begun to function as it should, while Inter-State Council had been set up to go into disputes between States.

The V.P. Singh government obtained as many as five constitutional amendments from the parliament.[4] All land reform legislations are included in the 9th Schedule of the Constitution which had been a long standing and long denied demand of the progressive elements of the country. Most of the issues were so important that not even the Congress (I) opposition dared to oppose them, though during its own regime it studiously avoided acting on them. On the other hand some of the National Front government's policies like the wholesale change of Governors immediately after assuming office and attempted coup in Karnataka in October 1990, when the Congress (I) was in the process of changing the leader, showed it up as no less manipulative and unprincipled than the regime it replaced.[5]

In Punjab, the initial promise of healing touch and quick solution soon came to nought. The situation in Kashmir worsened sharply during its term mainly because of the insensitive handling in the early stages. Punjab and Kashmir are of course inherited problems, but the National Front government also tried to deal with them with inherited means and ideas. The openness and inclusiveness V.P. Singh initiated in Punjab was hijacked by a few hundred terrorists.[6] The desperate killings of innocent people by the terrorists succeeded in throwing the new regime in Delhi to the beaten track of employing superior force to flush out what looks like, but is in most cases not, an inferior force. Hence extension of President's rule in Punjab with a constitutional amendment without any guarantee that after six months elections will be held.

In Kashmir, the total alienation from India has been taking place since the death of Sheikh Abdulla. There is no doubt that the solution could be achieved only through political rather than coercive methods. Thus Prime Minister V.P. Singh gave the additional charge of J & K affairs to the Railway Minister George Fernandes. Unfortunately, the government faltered because of the polar differences between the BJP's and the Left Front's approach to Kashmir.[7] The controversy occurred over the appointment of Jag

Mohan as Governor of Jammu & Kashmir, was a best example of the different perspectives of the Left and the BJP regarding Jammu & Kashmir. The Left always favoured a political solution to the problem while the BJP's stand reflects its Hindu communalist point of view and hints at settlement through force and compulsion. All party conferences also failed. Thus fearing the Pakistani threat to Kashmir, the National Front government increased 10 percent budgetory allotment to Defence. This was a grave violation of V.P.Singh's election time promise to lower defence expenditure to find more resources for poverty alleviation.

In Assam also the law and order situation worsened during the period. The activities of United Liberation Front of Asom and the inefficiency to tackle the tribal issues by the Asom Gana Parishath (AGP)[8] government due to its internal contradictions also created problems to the V.P. Singh government. Finally, in the economic front the 'liberalisation policy' of the government was severely criticised by the Left Front and by the Janata Dal leaders like Devilal and Chandrasekhar. The uncontrolled price rise also contributed to the woes of the fragile coalition.

From Crisis to Crisis

The National Front government which V.P. Singh headed had been described as one going from one crisis to another. Right from the beginning of the formation of Janata Dal and National Front, one of the senior leaders of the party, S. Chandrasekhar had not accepted the leadership of V.P. Singh. He had viewed Singh as an upstart who had done the right thing to be always on the side of power. There was some truth in it, that V. P. Singh was a political child of Indira Gandhi, so flourished like no other leader during the Emergency. Therefore, Chandrasekhar decided to contest for the parliamentary party leadership of Janata Dal and National Front. But the murky trick played on 1st December 1989, in the selection of V.P. Singh as the leader of Janata Dal was beyond the gaze of the public. What happened on that day was a political drama and as was known. V.P. Singh proposed Devilal's name for the post of leader and naturally Chandrasekhar seconded it but Devilal declined to take up the responsibility and instead suggested

V.P. Singh as the leader.[9] The 'Raja' and the 'Tau' thus connived to outmaneuver Chandrasekhar.

Just after the inception of the new government, the appointment of Jag Mohan as Governor of Jammu & Kashmir perpetuated a controversy on political lines, which have already explained earlier. At that crucial juncture on 27th February 1990, the next major crisis hit the Janata Dal. It was the day, the fall of the National Front government started. At the infancy itself, the power plumbers within the Janata Dal struck a bleeding blow at the moral foundation of the new regime. Devilal, who was one of the master builders of the Janata Dal, and whom V.P. Singh had adequately rewarded with the office of Deputy Prime Minister, set a much higher price for the family ownership of the state of Haryana than the survival of the alternative regime ushered in only three months before.[10] His resignation in March over the issue of his son Om Prakash Chautala's continuation as Haryana Chief Minister,[11] despite the massive rigging and booth capturing at Meham, rocked the fragile boat of the National Front government. This happened when the National Front was celebrating the electoral success and formation of Janata Dal governments in Orissa, Uttar Pradesh, Bihar and Gujarat.

The request of the Janata Dal to the Election Commission for a re-poll in Meham was interpreted by Devilal as the result of a "conspiracy of the capitalist media and rootless leaders against the rural and mass based political leader."[12] Devilal gave a political colour to his family ambitions and gave the reason for his resignation at the anti-rural and anti-farmer stand of the government. He demanded 50 percent of the budgetary allocations to the rural sector. But Devilal soon realised that he cannot muster the necessary support at that time and took back his resignation on the request of Janata Dal Chief Ministers. Soon after Prime Minister V.P.Singh awarded the rural electorate with the budget allocation of 49 percent of the exchequer for rural sector.[13]

The Election Commission countermanded the Meham by-election and the consequent polling in May 1990 witnessed more violence, the murder of one of the candidates and the countermanding of the election once again. Political compulsions from within and outside the Janata Dal, forced Chautala to resign and Banarasi Das Gupta became the Chief Minister of Haryana. In June 1990, Chautala won another assembly by-election from Darba Kalan and on 12th July he was sworn in again as Chief Minister. The havoc broke loose in the Janata Dal and several ministers including Arun Nehru, Arif Mohammad Khan and Satyapal Malik resigned over the Chautala issue. On 14th July V.P. Singh handed over his resignation to the party president S.R. Bommai.[14] Within a couple of days not only the Janata Dal, but also the National Front reaffirmed their unmistakable support to the leadership of V.P. Singh. Once again Chautala was stepped down. A marginalised Devilal faltered again by sending across to the Prime Minister's office a forged letter, implicating Arun Nehru in the Bofors gun deal. Soon afterwards in an interview Devilal called the Prime Minister as spineless. Both these issues ranged the entire party against Devilal. His isolation was complete and V.P. Singh sacked his deputy on 1st August 1990, for violating the canons of "collective responsibility".[15]

Devilal expected to fight his unceremonious ouster through his Kisan rally on 9th August. However, the Prime Minister took all by surprise on 7th August by announcing the acceptance of the Mandal Commission recommendations reserving 27 percent of the central government and public sector jobs for the backward castes/classes.[16] Even though the prime aim of V.P. Singh was to undercut the base of Devilal, the decision made long standing repercussions because in his attempts to make a permanent political constituency, V.P. Singh gave social change in India a new dimension.

The V. P. Singh government's decision to resurrect and implement the Mandal Commission recommendations, threw BJP into a panic. The decision had drawn significant lower caste support to the V. P. Singh dispensation. Even though lower caste had hardly been a BJP electoral bastion at that time, the prospects of their large scale identification with another political party was a source of concern.[17] Even though the BJP leaders deny this in public, the reality is that the party saw the report as a dire threat to its very existence. The 27 per cent reservations for the backward castes and classes augured to sunder BJP's vote banks by dividing the Hindu vote.[18] Thus the BJP decided to wield the Ayodhya sword with ruthless determination and Advani started the Rath Yatra with the Viswa Hindu Parishad declared *Kar Seva* at the Ram Janma Bhoomi-Babri Masjid site on 30th October 1990.

BJP Withdraws Support to V.P. Singh Government

The cracks between the BJP and the National Front government had started developing several months ago. The Prime Minister had gone back on his assurance on granting statehood to Delhi and he had replaced the Jammu & Kashmir Governor Jag Mohan who was backed by the BJP. The Prime Minister also declared prophet Mohammad's birth day as a holiday from the Red Fort during his independence day address to the nation. It is true that on the plea of implementing the Mandal Commission Report, V.P. Singh sought to damage the natural constituency of the BJP which comprised the upper and the middle castes. Thus the idea of Advani's rath yatra from Somanath to Ayodhya was based on the old RSS tactic of whipping up religious passions to end caste conflicts.[19] Keeping this in mind the emergent meeting of the National Executive Committee of the BJP declared that if the rath yatra was stopped or attempts were made to prevent *kar seva* in Ayodhya, the party would be constrained to withdraw support to the V.P. Singh government. This became a reality with the arrest of L. K. Advani at Samsthipur in Bihar on 23rd October, 1990.

The BJP, two days before the arrest of Advani, had rejected the three point formula forwarded by the government through a Presidential Ordinance to take over the disputed site in Ayodhya and refer the possession case to the Supreme Court. The BJP also precipitated the process of political polarisation by claiming to be a nationalist party while branding all others opposed to it as "pseudo secularists." Thus the combined moves of the BJP and the Viswha Hindu Parishad (VHP), by openly declaring that they would not accept any court verdict on Ram Janma Bhoomi- Babri Masjid controversy threatened the secular foundation of Indian polity and heightened the insecurity of the minorities. With the withdrawal of support by the BJP, the triangular arrangement exposed its artificiality that the centrist coalition, the National Front in power with the outside support of the Left and Right, in the hope that it would keep aloft the banner of non-Congressism. Prime Minister V.P. Singh requested the President to call a special session of the Lok Sabha on 7th November to seek a vote of confidence in the House.

Janata Dal Faces Vertical Split

The long-standing dissidence in the Janata Dal which had surfaced in September 1990, led by Yaswant Sinha, a Rajya Sabha member and stoked by Chandrasekhar, culminated in 29 Dal MPs signing a memorandum demanding V.P. Singh's resignation. They charged that V. P. Singh had failed to stem the rot of Mandal violence and failures on Punjab and Kashmir. However, once again the Janata Dal and the National Front parliamentary parties reaffirmed their confidence in V.P. Singh. But, after Mr. Singh lost his majority with the withdrawal of support by the BJP, the dissidents met on 5th November at Devi Lal's house and elected S. Chandrasekhar as their leader.[20] The meeting expelled V.P. Singh from the leadership of the Janata Dal Parliamentary Party.[21] The dissidents formed a new party called Janata Dal (Socialist) and later Devilal became the president of the new party.

On the other hand, the Janata Dal Parliamentary Party on the same day expelled Chandrasekhar and twenty four of his Lok Sabha Colleagues and five Rajya Sabha members from the Jnana Dal for "anti-party activities and colliding with the Congress (I) openly".[22] However, Devilal and some of his associates were not suspended on that day. This was a fruitless tactical move for following the suspension, Lok Sabha Speaker Rabi Ray on 6th November, ordered the twenty-five expelled Janata Dal Lok Sabha MPs to sit as unattached members of the House. Meanwhile some members of the V.P.Singh Ministry resigned and joined the dissidents.[23] As a final step, the 1979 drama was staged once again when Chandrasekhar met the Congress (I) President Rajiv Gandhi and they[24] [agree]d to work together.[25]

On 7th November 1990, for the first time in the history of independent India, a Ministry was voted out by the Lok Sabha.[26] The Prime Minister V.P. Singh, seeking vote of confidence from the Lok Sabha said that there will be no "sanctity or political legitimacy" if a "splinter group" is given the responsibility. Appealing to the members to vote according to their conscience in the interest of the country's unity, integrity and secularism Mr. Singh said that the issue was not of a government but that of principles. He said that the BJP had never made the construction of the Rama temple in Ayodhya a condition for extending support to the National Front government when it was formed. Referring to the proposal for "national government", Mr. Singh said it would not be possible to join hands with the BJP, which considered itself above the Constitution and law. He said that the main issue was not the rath yatra or the *kar seva* but the basic thrust of this government taking up programmes for the backward and depressed classes which was responsible for the present crisis. In the attempts to defeat his government, he said "the anger at the implementation of the Mandal Commission recommendations are positively hidden there".[27] The Congress (I) President and leader of the Opposition Rajiv Gandhi, charged the National Front government with total failure on all fronts and said that it had unleashed "divisive forces to encourage communalism and casteism"[28] The BJP President L.K. Advani demanded fresh election to the Lok Sabha.[29]

Finally, when voting took place the vertical split in the Janata Dal was reflected along with the realignment of political forces. Devilal and Chandrasekhar joined together along with the Congress (1) and the BJP. V.P. Singh was supported by 82 members of the Janata Dal, the members of the Left Front and some of the small political parties. The social chaos following the Mandal decision and the system's failure after the BJP rath yatra began, only made matters easy for V.P. Singh's political enemies. The fear spread among the Janata Dal MPs that their leaders might be heading for mid-term elections to cash in on the Mandal factor also helped Chandrasekhar and Devilal. The MPs had been elected less than a year ago and did not want to go through the test again so soon. Chandrasekhar played host to all those ranged against

V.P. Singh, since the inception of the new ministry. Soon his constituency became the disgruntled factional bosses of the party and the following they commanded in parliament. It is no secret that they hobnobbed with the Congress (I).

Table 7.1

Voting Pattern on the Motion of Confidence in the V.P. Singh Ministry

For	151	Against	356
Janata Dal	82	Congress (a)	193
Left Front	52	BJP	85
Jhakhand Mukti Morcha	3	Janata Dal (Rebel) / Unattached Members	30 / 25
Telugu Desam	2	AIADMK	11
˙IUML	2	National conference	3
Associate Members of the National Front	2	Shiv Sena	4
Congress (S)	1	Hindu Mahasabha	1
Indian People's Front	1	Kerala Congress (M)	1
Marxist Co-ordination committee	1	Independents	3
MGP (Goa)	1		
Sikkim Sangram Parishad	1	Note: Out of the effective strength of 524 in the Lok Sabha 11 were absent (NF-3, Cong ((I)-1, BJP-1, GNLF-1, Akali Dal-2, Independents-2) and 6 abstained (BSP-3, Akali Dal-2, Independent-1	
Majilis-e-Ittehad Musilmeen	1		
Independent	1		
Mr. Abdul Samad (Cong. (I)- Ind)			

* After voting for the V.P. Singh Ministry the Muslim league later decided to support the Chandrasekhar Ministry.

Source: The Hindu, 9 November, 1990.

After the resignation of the V.P. Singh Ministry, President R.Venkataraman, inquired of the Congress (I), then BJP and the Left Front, whether they "will be able and willing to form a viable government". They were not willing and then on 10th November 1990, S. Chandrasekhar sworn in as the Prime Minister of India with the support of the Congress (I) and AIADMK from outside.[30] It is clear that the new government formed by the split-away Janata Dal (S) depends totally for its survival on the mercy of the Congress (I).

The realignment of the forces at the centre had its repercussions in the various Janata Dal- BJP ruled states. In Gujarat the dissident Janata Dal Chief Minister Chimanbhai Patel, survived on the support of the Congress (I) days before Chandrasekar was sworn in as Prime Minister. In Rajasthan and Madhya Pradesh the Janata Dal withdrew its support to the BJP Chief Ministers, but they survived with the help of the Janata Dal dissidents. In Uttar Pradesh after much hesitation, the Congress (I) and the Janata Dal (S) joined together for the survival of the Chief Minister Mulayam Singh Yadav. Only in Bihar, the Janata Dal Chief Minister got the confidence vote with the support of the leftists and the Jharkhand Mukthi Morcha.

The 1996 United Front alliance was primarily a post-election coalition. Thus the circumstances in which the National Front came apart ensured that parties could not quickly come together again. The BJP's programme of Hindu cultural nationalism strengthened the secular -communal divide in the party system and drew clear lines of political engagement. The Left and what remained of the National Front were therefore no longer willing to do business with the BJP. For the BJP, the other backward class (OBC) agenda of the Janata Dal and its partners was a divisive instrument countering its cultural- integrationist strategy.[31] With these developments, the emerging pattern of political polarisation is clearly visible in the political horizon- the Congress (I) and it's allies on the Centre, the BJP- Shiv Sena combine on the Right and the Janata Dal-Left Front combination striving to form a Left-of-Centre government at the National level.

Notes and References:

1   K.K. Katyal, 'Craving for a Change' *The Hindu*, 4 December, 1989.

2   See, Gail Omvedt, 'The Anti-caste Movement and the Discourse of Power', Niraja Gopal Jayal (ed.), Democracy in India, New Delhi, Oxford University Press, 2001.

3. B.Muralidhar Reddy - Interview with V.P.Singh,   *Front-line*, November 24-December 7, 1990, p. 19.

4. The Amendments are: The Constitution (Sixty second Amendment) Act (1989)-amending Article 334; (Sixty third Amendment) Act-(1989)-amending Article 356 (Omitting proviso to CL (5) and omitting Article 359. A; (Sixty fourth Amendment) Act-(1990) Amending Article. 356; (Sixty Fifth Amendment) Act (1990)-amending Article 338; and (Sixty sixth Amendment) Act - (1990) inserting entries 203 to 257 in the Ninth Schedule; for details see D.D. *Basu, Introduction to the Constitution of India* , New Delhi, 1990.

5. In Karnataka the Congress (I) Chief Minister V.H. Paril was asked to quite by the Congress (I) Party President Rajiv Gandhi. Patil refused to budge. Then in October on the report of the Governor Bhanu Pratap Singh, the National Front government dismissed the government and put the Assembly in suspended animation. It was alleged that it was an attempted coup by the centre to scuttle the Congress (I) rule. However, Bangarappa was unanimously elected as the new leader ad sworn in as Chief Minister of Karnataka on October 17, 1990.

6. Babani Sen Gupta, 'Limits of Consensus Politics' *Economic and Political Weekly*, April 7, 1990, p. 700.

7. The Left parties are always in favour of the special status given to Jammu & Kashmir in the Constitution of India (clause (1) of Article-370) while the BJP is fighting for the deletion of this constitutional provision.

8. *The Indian Express*, 2 December, 1989.

9. Babani Sen Gupta, *Ibid.*, p. 701.

10. Chautala was put into the cradle of Chief Minister, by Devilal when he abdicated the post for deputy Prime Minister ship. Chautala was not a member of the Haryana legislature, and thus contested from Meham.

11. *Onlooker*, November 15, 1990, p.16.

12. *The Hindu*, March 19, 1990.

13. *Ibid.*, 15 July, 1990.

14. *Ibid.*, 2 August, 1990.

15. In his efforts to implement the Mandal report, V.P.Singh had staunch lieutenants the Union Labour Minister, Ram Vilas Paswan and the Textiles Ministers Sharad Yadav, Bihar Chief Minister Laloo Prasad Yadav and UP Chief Minister Mulayam Singh Yadav. The Left Front also supported the Prime Minister.

16. Pankaj Pachauri, 'An Election Gamble' *India Today*, November 15, 1990, p.31.

17. Sumit Ganguly and Rahul Mukerji, *India Since 1980*, New Delhi, Cambridge University Press, 2011, p. 129.

18. Pankaj Vora, 'The BJP Game Plan', *The Hindu Weekly Edition*, 11 November, 1990.

19. The meeting was attended by Janata Dal leaders like-Asok sen, Yaswant Sinha , Raj Mangal Pandey and the Gujarat Chief Minister Chimanbhai Patel.

20. *The Hindu*, 6 November, 1990.

21. *Ibid.*,

22 The Ministers who resigned were Maneka Gandhi, Manubari Kathadia, Jnaneshwar Mistra, Subodhkhan Sahay, Usha Singh and Jagdip Dhankar.

23. In 1979 the actors were Charan Singh and Indira Gandhi.

24. *The Hindu*, 7 November 1990.

25. *Ibid.*, 8 November 1990.

26. *Ibid.*,

27 *Ibid.*

28 After voting for the V. P. Singh Ministry the Muslim League later decided to support the Chandrasekhar Ministry.

29 *The Hindu*, 9 November 1990.

30 *The Hindu*,11 November 1990.

31 K. K. Kailash, 'Competition and Coalition Formation in the New Party System', in E. Sridharan (ed.), Coalition Politics in India: Selected Issues at the Centre and the States, New Delhi, Academic Foundation, 2014, p.94.

8

Left Politics: Retrospect and Prospect

The 1980 Lok Sabha election witnessed the coming together of the two mainstream Communist Parties in India. After more than a decade of rivalry and bitterness the Communist Party of India (CPI) and the Communist Party of India (Marxist) -CPI (M) accepted the historical necessity of a radical democratic platform around which the Left and the radical democratic forces in the country can purposefully unite for mass struggles and for mass action. They felt that, only through such a united mass movement and mass action can the Indian Left play its effective role in the present national situation and bring about necessary shifts in the political balance of forces to take the country towards socialism. With this political development in the Indian political arena, they expected that the future of Left and democratic forces is seems to be clear and bright. It is interesting to analyse the Left politics during the period and factors which led to the coming together of the Communist parties which ultimately led to the formation of the Left and Democratic Front in Kerala[1] and the Left Front[2] in West Bengal and at the national level.

The Left in India comprises two strands - the Marxian and the Left nationalist. The Marxian strand represents mainly by the CPI, the CPI (M), and the various CPI (ML) groups, generally called-Naxalites. Most of the Naxalite groups later joined together under the Maoist umbrella. The Left nationalist strand were represented by the Samyukta Socialist Party (SSP) and Praja Socialist Party (PSP) and now the Revolutionary Socialist Party (RSP) and the All India Forward Bloc (AIFB).

Historically the Communist Party of the India formally came into being at an All India Conference which met from the end of December 1925 to the beginning of January 1926 at Kanpur.[3] Though the Indian Communists officially adopted parliamentary democracy as a means to achieve socialism at the Amritsar Congress of the Communist Party of India in 1957,[4] divergence regarding strategy and tactics surfaced only after the split of 1964. While the Socialists got divided in the fifties and fell prey to irrational anti-communism, the Communists within whose rank ideological warfare had been going on, got split following the Sino-Soviet Schism, the Sino-Indian conflict and on the issue of tactical alliance with the national bourgeoisie and it's political manifestation - the Indian National Congress.

Theoretically, both the CPI and the CPI (M) believe in a two-state revolution[5] that is, a democratic revolution to complete the anti-imperialist and anti-feudal task as a prelude to the Socialist Revolution. Thus their starting point of analysis is the same. But the CPI believed in the national democratic revolution and advocated that 'no national democratic front would be real unless the vast mass following of the Congress, especially the progressive sections would have their place.'[6] Following the split, for essentially pragmatic reasons the CPI and the CPI (M) had some measure of accommodation in 1967 and 1968, but from 1968 onwards their paths rapidly diverged. Objectively, the CPI played in the hands of Indira Gandhi and sabotaged Left unity. While saying itself 'unity and struggle' policy in practice it remembered only 'unity' and forgot about 'struggle'. In the name of fighting against right reaction the CPI supported authoritarianism and lost its credibility in the process. The role played by the CPI was clearly visible during the period of Emergency from June 1975 to March 1977, and from the severe blow which it received in the March 1977 Lok Sabha elections.

As against the CPI policy of 'unity and struggle' the CPI(M) advocated People's Democracy and opposed any collaboration with the ruling Congress party. During the Emergency it played only a passive role against authoritarianism but vehemently criticised the 'dynastic dictatorship' of Indira Gandhi. In the 1977 elections the

CPI (M) joined hands with the Janata Party and the result was that the CPI (M) could barely retain its strength in the Lok Sabha. In 1989both parties supported the Janata Dal and the United Front.

It is one of the ironies of political life that in a country of poor people like ours the Left and other progressive elements should have wasted long years on differences that could have waited to be sorted out. It should be noted that the Communist movement took deep roots and maintained its position only in three states of West Bengal, Kerala and Tripura and some parts of Bihar and Andhra Pradesh. The failure of Communist parties in this respect is due to many obvious reasons primarily, the splits which occurred in 1964, as pointed out earlier and also in 1968, by which large sections of the workers and landless labourers from the CPI(M) parted away from it, especially in the states of West Bengal, Andhra Pradesh, Bihar and Kerala and formed the Communist Party of India (Marxist-Leninist).

What set apart the CPI (ML) from the other Leftist parties is their ideological commitment of the thought of Mao-Tse-tung and the rejection of the Soviet Union as a socialist country. They called the Post- Stalin Soviet Union as the Social Imperialists. The CPI (ML) rejected any hope to bring about changes in society within the present parliamentary framework. Their aim is to mobilise the landless and the small peasantry and organise guerilla warfare to seize power. The Naxalbari and Srikakalum armed uprisings in West Bengal and Andhra Pradesh and various other armed rebellions in different parts of the country in the sixties and seventies of this century were under the banner of the CPI (ML). At present most of the CPI (ML) groups are in different parts of the country merged with CPI(Maoist) and active through their cultural and human rights organisations.

Another reason for the set back of the Communist movement in India was that they have advanced an agenda for social transformation in India with little reflective thought on the specificity of Indian social formation...a refusal yo engage with the concrete conditions of the concrete situation. This was manifest in the way they have handled issues of tradition, identity, culture, communities and castes.[7] The caste-class dichotomy is still a problematic for the communists to theorise. Further, in the absence of proletarian class consciousness, and social awareness, the monetary gains of the working class are also liquidated. Since the Communist movement is linked with the working class, it must be educated to temper its economic demands and ensure that it is in no case alienated from the other toiling sections of society. Thus, while criticising always the "right revisionism" of the CPI and the "left adventurism" of the CPI (ML) groups, the CPI (M) in its Salkia Plenum document (1978) said; "our mass leaders are not conscious of their responsibility and our party as a whole has failed to develop the elementary class consciousness of the proletariat into socialist consciousness and attract large numbers to the party organisations".[8]

Another important aspect in this context is the failure on the part Left parties and groups to build the movement among the masses, with large and important areas completely left out of calculation. They failed to cultivate the support of the key classes in a caste ridden society. This is mainly because of the most opportunistic role played by the CPI and the CPI (M) in the recent past after they immersed in electoral gains only. Nothing creditably is gained and much is lost by thinking in terms of alliances and adjustments for the sake of a few seats, here and there.[9]

Another important problem confronting the Communists is that the Hindi heartland containing the poorest and most backward sections of our people was largely neglected. Leftist influence in this area which is decisive in the context of national politics has been less than nominal, and the vested interests in collaboration with obscurantist elements gained control. The absence of cadre building and organisation of mass struggles on crucial issues must be held responsible for this situation. Former CPI(M) General Secretary E.M.S. Namboodiripad in an interview, admitted the drawbacks and failures of the movement and pointed out the causes. According to him the hold of capitalist-reactionary doctrines and ideas of the people is chiefly responsible for this failure. Religious and communal feelings also have contributed towards checking communist growth. He agreed that the communist leadership has failed in instilling in the people an awareness of those tendencies and in mobilising their opposition against them.[10]

The newly formed Left Democratic Front in Kerala, barring the communal parties like the Kerala Congresses and Muslim League, the support the Communist parties extended to the V.P. Singh government in fighting the communalism of BJP and Viswa Hindu Parishad in the Babri Masjid-Ram Janmabhoomi controversy and the willingness to accept the implementation of the Mandal Commission report are all their belated attempts to come into terms with the Indian political realities. It must be an eye opener to the Left and democratic forces in the country that the decision to implement the Mandal Commission report, ultimately brought down the National Front government. In this sense, the most difficult Indian riddle which the Communists and other progressive elements in Indian society have to solve is the intertwining of caste and class, of deciding how far to carry their fight against casteism and communalism and how to make use of the castes as short cut. An understanding of the process of interaction between the 'base' and 'superstructure'[11] in the Indian socio-economic milieu is not so simple as in western social systems. Social revolution in India demands structural changes in a tradition oriented developing society and necessitates the class struggle at economic and cultural level for "the Marxist intellectual tradition, the relation of the state to class struggle continues to the present day to be a central polemical issue".[12]

During the Emergency, with the merger of the socialists in the Janata Party, the only two major Leftist parties available as identifiable national political entities in the parliamentary system were the CPI and the CPI (M). Till then both have been projecting the idea of unity of all Left and democratic forces, beginning with "unity in action"[13] meaning the launching of joined mass struggles on local and national issues directly affecting the working people-rural and urban. Though the idea of Left and democratic unity has been discussed vigorously for sometime, it did not reach in a practical shape till the 1980 Lok Sabha elections. This is mainly due to CPI's attachment to the ruling Congress party and to a certain extent CPI(M)'s proximity to the Janata Party.

Conversely, some political analysts argue that, in a way the CPI policy of 'unity and struggle' with the Congress, contributed itself to the Left and democratic unity by the radicalisation of a large section of Congressmen, making them stand against Indira Gandhi. They were prepared to accept an alliance with the communist parties. An outstanding but short-lived example to this process can be sighted in the LDF ministry in Kerala, which came to power in 1980.[14] A recent and more fruitful example of this type of 'radicalisation' can be sighted in the decisive role played by the Left along with the Janata Dal, during and after the 1989 Lok Sabha elections. Later, in the fight against casteism and communalism the Left has got an ally in the dominant faction of the Janata Dal.

Towards Unity and Co-operation

As pointed our earlier, the 1977 Lok Sabha elections gave the CPI a severe jolt. Many, but not everybody in the leadership and ranks realised that the party had committed a grave crime against Left and democratic unity. At the 11th Congress at Bhatinda, it recorded that "our party's independent image was blurred and it become identified with the then ruling Congress Party".[15] It confessed that it should not have supported Internal Emergency.[16] While every group in the CPI professed to stand by the slogan of Left and democratic unity, there were sharp differences on who should be regarded as Left or democratic. These differences existed in the top leadership also- one section is represented by C. Rajeswara Rao and Bhupesh Gupta and the other section by S.A. Dange. After the Chikmagalur by-election, Dange publicly gloated over Indira Gandhi's victory and made abrasive comments on the CPI (M)'s support to the Janata candidate. The CPI Central Executive publicly censured him for such grave violation of party discipline. There is no doubt that Dange had gone against the CPI's policy decided at Bhatinda, which spoke of "supreme importance of exploring all possible areas of agreement between the CPI and the CPI (M)".[17] At that moment with the new coalition in Kerala and all over the country with the Marxists, Rajeswara Rao and Bhupesh Gupta seemed to be in the right path. They rejected any truck with

Indira Gandhi and her party. Consequently, the supporters of Dange formed a new party known as All India Communist Party (AICP).

Following the Bhatinda Congress (1978) of the CPI and Jullundar Congress (1978) of the CPI(M), the leaders of the two parties met and discussed the modus operandi for building a Left alternative. After this meeting, in most of the states the two Communist parties have taken steps for joined actions through their mass organisations. This is because, as the CPI General Secretary said that the "Communist and other like minded parties could have a significant role in building a Left alternative if they set aside petty considerations and provide bold leadership to the people."[18]

The CPI (M) regards itself independent of the Communist Party of Soviet Union (CPSU) and the Communist Party of China (CPC). The CPI, on the other hand, had strong links with the CPSU and was at that time divided on the issue of following the Moscow line. The CPI (M) however had not criticised Soviet foreign policy except certain aspects of Soviet policies about India. In contrast it had differed strongly from, and condemned several foreign policy decisions of the Chinese People's Republic, especially those affecting geographically close to India. Of late the Soviet leadership restored party level relations with the CPI (M) in 1983. The CPI, on the other hand, has stood firmly behind Moscow in its pervasive conflict with Peking. However, the leadership of the CPI has been urging to separate domestic politics from India's relations with the USSR. It continues to oppose Congress (I), despite the friendship existing between the CPSU and the Congress Party. These developments also contributed towards the Left unity.

Following the developments towards a Left and Democratic Front in Kerala, the CPI (M) had demanded the dissolution of the Kerala Legislative Assembly headed by the CPI Chief Minister P.K. Vasudevan Nair. As a retaliation to the offensive which brought down the Kerala government headed by E.M.S. Namboodiripad in October 1969, the CPI (M) had also demanded fresh elections as a precondition for forging a new Left Front[19] The CPI was reluctant and wanted the CPI (M) to join the United Front. However, in the 1979 Panchayat elections the CPI met the debacle and this new development compelled the CPI leadership to quit the United Front, without an advice to dissolve the Legislature. Meanwhile, the Janata government collapsed and Charan Singh became Prime Minister with the support of the Congress, the Congress (I) and the Leftists. Later the Congress (I) withdrew its support and the Charan Singh Ministry collapsed and the seventh Lok Sabha elections took place in 1980. In Kerala, the new ministry headed by Muslim League leader C.H. Mohammad Koya was also collapsed due to the shift in support of the Kerala Congress (M). The Congress led by A.K. Antony came over to join the CPI (M) Front in November 1979. Thus fresh elections took place in Kerala along with the 1980 Lok Sabha elections.

At the national level, the election strategy of the Communists was a two pronged one, aiming at the development of Indian communist power as a decisive force and to defeat the Congress (I)- RSS controlled authoritarian-communal forces.[20] The result was better performance by the two Communist parties in all India level and the victory of CPI(M) led Left and Democratic Front in Kerala. Thus the alliance of the two Communist parties along with the R.S.P. and Forward Bloc, established a powerful platform of the healthy and patriotic trends. It also proved that the social roots of this power reach deep in the rural classes in the case of the CPI(M), while for the CPI, they are mostly confined to urban workers and middle classes.[21]

At the 1984 Lok Sabha elections also, the Left Front followed a policy for the unity of Left and democratic forces. However, in Kerala the LDF lost most of the Lok Sabha seats. Meanwhile, at the end of its first term of office in 1982, the Left Front in West Bengal sought a renewed mandate, two years after Indira Gandhi's sweeping national parliamentary victory of 1980. The result was triumphant-the Left won 81 per cent of the seats in West Bengal Assembly on a resounding 52.6 per cent share of the vote.

In the 1989 Lok Sabha elections, the Left Front stood side by side with the newly formed Janata Dal and National Front. At the national level the National Front had an alliance with the BJP on one hand and the Left on the other. However, the Left had no electoral understanding with the BJP. The election results led to the formation of the minority National Front government with the support of the BJP and the Left Front from outside. Even after the withdrawal of support by the BJP and the collapse of the V.P. Singh Government, the Left Front and the Janata Dal are fighting the communalist and authoritarian elements in Indian society.

Table 8.1

Communist Performance in Lok Sabha Elections - 1952-89

Party	CPI		CPI(M)	
Year	Seats won	Percentage cote	Seats won	Percentage vote
1952	16	3.1	-	-
1957	27	8.9	-	-
1962	29	9.9	-	-
1967	23	5.1	19	4.4
1971	7	2.8	22	4.3
1980	11	2.6	36	6.1
1984	6	2.7	22	5.8
*1989	12	2.7	33	6.4

* In 1989 the total seals won by the Left Front is 52 (RSP-4 and Forward Bloc-3) and Percentage of vote is 10.3.

During the historical period discussed in this study, the stubborn resilience of centrism in Indian politics has always been the despair of the Left parties. However, the failure of the Congress system and the failure of the Janata and National Front experiments, even though they are qualitatively different, has opened up immense possibilities of advance for the Left forces in India. In order to utilise these possibilities most fruitfully, it is incumbent on the Left to make a sober objective analysis of the

Indian socio-economic realities, freed from all pre conceived political prejudices and devise a correct strategy of united action to meet the challenge posed. The two important challenges before the Left parties in India are: (i) the changes in the economy brought about by a new technology ushered in by the neo-liberal global order that has changed the composition of both the industrial working class and the professional middle classes, on the one hand; and (ii) the growing self-assertion by hitherto ignored oppressed communities and sections of the population, which are being marginalised by the impact of this neo-liberal economic order on the other.[21] It is these changes that call for the strategy of revolutionary transformation in India. There can be no short cut to social revolution in India. Those who attempt to short-circuit this path by dogmatic formulae and cliques or by unprincipled parliamentary manoeuvres will come to grief and will have to learn things the hard way.

Notes and References:

1   At present the LDF in Kerala consists of the CPI(M), the CPI, the SDP, the Janata Dal, the Congress (A) and the Lok Dal.

2   The Left Front in West Bengal and also at national level comprises of the four left Parties-the CPI (M), the CPI, the RSP and the Forward Bloc.

3   N.E. Balaram, *A Short History of the Communist Party of India*, Trivandrum, 1967, p. 8.

4   D.R. Goyal, 'Confrontation with Democracy', *Seminar* No. 127 March 1970, p. 40.

5   Mohan Ram, 'The Compromise Game', *Seminar*, No. 362, October 1989, pp. 24-25.

6   T.J. Nossiter, *Marxist State Governments in India: Politics, Economics and Society*, London, 1988, p.24.

7   Valerian Rodrigues, 'The Communist Parties in India', in Peter Ronald deSouza (eds.) *India's Political Parties*, New Delhi, Sage Publications, 2006, p.245.

8   Tarun Ganguly, 'The CPI(M)'s Real Politic', *Sunday*, 4 November 1979, p.31.

9   Amarjit Chandran, 'North After the Rout', *Economic and Political Weekly*, 19 January 1930, p. 1185.

10 *The Kerala Sabdam Weekly*,13 December 1979, p.6.

11 In the Indian context, Antonio Gramsci's concept of "Hegemony" is relevant. See his *Selections from the Prison Note Books,* London -1971.

12 Gabriel A. Almond, 'The Return to the State', *American Political Science Review*, 82: 3, September 1988, p. 856.

13 C.N. Chittaranjan, 'Will the Communists of India Unite?', *The Illustrated Weekly of India,* January 7-13, 1979, p. 18.

14 Besides the three Left Parties CPI (M), CPI and RSP, the Left Democratic Front Ministry included the Mani and Pillai factions of the Kerala Congress, the All India Muslim league (none of which qualified for the label's 'Democratic' or 'Left', in Marxian terms) and the Congress (Urs) headed by A.K. Antony.

15 Sumit Mitra, 'The Past Catches Up', *India Today*, 16-31 March 1979, p. 33.

16 K.K. Katyal, 'Towards Communist Reconciliation?', *The Hindu*, 10 April 1978.

17 Ranjit Roy, 'The CPI Left Alienated', *Sunday*, 4 November 1979, p.29.

18 *Link*: India's New Magazine, 14 May 1978.

19 *The Indian Express*, 17 March 1979.

20 E.M.S. Nampoodiripad in an interview to *Kerala Sabdam Weekly*, 7 October 1979.

21 Babani Sen Gupta, 'Communist Power', *Seminar*, No. 248, April 1980, p. 35.

22 Sumanta Banerjee, 'Revolutionary Movements in a Post-Marxian Era', Economic and Political Weekly, Vol.XLVII (18), May 5, 2012, p.57.

9

Conclusion

For more than seven decades India has attempted a bold experiment in democracy and development. In a considerable measure the roots of India's democracy must be traced to the genius of the nationalist movement. India's outstanding nationalist leaders including Mohandas Gandhi, Jawaharlal Nehru and the architect of India's Constitution, Bhimrao Ambedkar, had shared a pluralistic vision of India. The liberal vision of the founding fathers, despite myriad challenges from within, has served India well. India's democratic trajectory, which has witnessed only two years of authoritarian rule (1975- 77) and complete civilian control over the military, is a significant achievement in the post- colonial world.[1]

In this respect elections in India can now be seen not merely as useful indicators but actually as the events through which the party system and hence in a measure the political system achieve their evolution. In 1989 as in 1977, the people voted for a broad based alliance of identities that had gone to them on a common platform of change. And for the vast majority of them, it was a change from the dominant regime and family at the Centre. However, the disintegration of the Janata experiment in 1979 and the collapse of the National Front Government in 1990 shows that the Indian democratic political process is still in the realm of basic experimenting and learning.

Historically, the single-party-dominant system in India was seen to be ended by coalescing all the political parties opposed to the Congress, in various patterns, these being mergers, alliances, electoral adjustments and joint action on specific issues. The successes of this strategy of a negative government making in the 1967 general elections was short lived, as the non-Congress multi-party coalitions which held power in nine states proved brittle. Yet the imposition of Emergency in 1975 resulting in the erosion of civil liberties and suppression of democrartic rights almost compelled the Opposition parties to try out the old formula once again with the new vision of Jayapraksh Narayan's 'total revolution'. So the Janata Party, hammered out by the unification of various centrist parties and the Jana Sangh was put into power amidst great euphoria. It too crumbled down within 27 months. Yet the question went on. Hence after another decade, a fresh trial was made and success was achieved for the third time and then followed the inevitable collapse.

The similarities between what had happened in 1979 and the developments occurred in 1990 is limited. In both cases it was the Opposition coalitions which came to power at the Centre was afflicted by the crisis. In the former occasion, it was triggered by the rift in the ruling Janata Party and in the latter it is the result of the differences in opinion over the main issues between the ruling party and one of its outside supporters. In both the cases, the ideological overtones were invested by differences arising from the policies of those who now constitute the BJP and on the previous occasion were in the Janata Party as the Jana Sangh constituent.

In 1979 it was essentially a class of personalities involving the then Prime Minister Moraji Desai and Charan Singh, the number two in the cabinet. However, the 'dual membership' issue provided the ideological base. The Janata government's performance during 1977-79, was much better than the Congress (I) governments in various fields. The Morarji government contributed much in re-establishing the democratic set up of the country damaged by the Emergency of 1975-77.

The National Front government which came into power in December 1989, had also done pretty well in the institutional and constitutional area of Indian political life, but pretty poorly in dealing with political disorder in the vital states of Kashmir and Punjab, even though they are inherited problems from the Congress (I) regime. As they came into power after the long family rule, the new regime was catapulted by popular enthusiasm to the pedestal of a value based alternative when compared to the personalised politics of decades. It shows a good deal of earnestness and good intentions in its approach to the formidable political and developmental tasks. But the Janata Dal/National Front government also sunk in an image of perpetual vulnerability and helplessness due to its internal contradictions. But as different from 1979 the coalition collapsed within one year, because of the glaring contradiction inherent in the uneasy alliance of a centrist force like the National Front with the two polar ends of the system the BJP and the Left Front.

The BJP's amiability vanished as it felt that its own base was likely to be fractured by the V.P. Singh government's decision to implement the Mandal Commission recommendations. The post-Mandal context saw a rapid souring of the atmosphere between the BJP and the National Front, with the BJP manipulating the Mandir-Masjid controversy as the flash point. The disturbances created by the urban middle classes following the government's decision to implement the Mandal Commission recommendations are widespread. But its significance lies in the fact that it is another important land mark in the country's march towards social change. Another manifestation of the problem created by the implementation of the Mandal recommendations is the encounter between Hinduism and modern politics based on liberalism and parliamentary democracy.[2]

Converting non-issues into issues to divert the attention of the masses from the basic issues is an age-old trick, the politicians play to gain popularity. The Mandal issue and the consequent 'rath yatra' of the BJP leader L.K. Advani, once again proved that the political parties and leaders in India could use this trick for political manipulation. In this respect, the matter for concern is not the future of the Janata Dal or for that matter the stability of the National Front government which crumbled down, but the very credibility of the public representatives and the respectability of democratic institutions.

The National Front had perforce to take upon itself the task of defending the political principle of secularism. In contrast, it is evident that the Congress (I) has been paying lip service to secularism without backing it up with any action. For instance, contrary to party President Rajiv Gandhi's assurance at the National Development Council meeting at Madras, in October 1990, L.K. Advani's Rath yatra was allowed in all Congress (I) ruling states like Maharashtra, Andhra Pradesh and Karnataka. Earlier in November 1989, the Congress (I) government at Delhi allowed the VHP for the foundation laying ceremony at the disputed place in Ayodhya despite the clear order of the court not to do so.

Thus it is evident that theV.P. Singh government's steadfast adherence to secularism in the Babri Masjid-Ram Janma Bhoomi controversy and a firm determination to ensure social justice through the implementation of the Mandal Commission recommendations are the main causes which brought the National Front government down to collapse. The most important positive result of all these developments is the political polarisation, marked by the coming together of the secular, democratic and Left forces. However, our greatest misfortune is that power and politics are not taken to the masses. In a country like India, gripped by severe socio-economic inequalities, the State could only acquire legitimacy as an instrument of socio-economic change, rather than of a passive reflex of the status quo. Implied in this process is a potentially gigantic redistribution of social, economic and state resources. Hence resistance to it is mobilised precisely by those political forces which stand for thinly- disguised, novel forms of authoritarian reconstruction of Indian state. Among these are the new fundamentalism of religious sects giving rise to perversions of old civilizations such as the Vishwa Hindu Parishad, the new found power of presumably 'cultural' organisations like the Rashtriya Swayam Sevak Sangh and the Jama-at-e-Islami and the growing communalism within secular politics.[3]

Once again we are faced with the choice of a secular democratic India on the one hand and an attempted subversion and high jacking of the nation by fascists masquerading as patriots, on the other.[4] A platform of social justice and secularism is the only possible basis for the continued existence of the Indian Union. The Indian Leftists is seen to be not in touch with the Indian social realities. However, along with the Janata Dal and other centrist and progressive elements in the country, they strived to build up a national platform of the Left, democratic and secular forces in the country. Only such a movement can protect the secularism and fundamental human values in our society, against the onslaught of communalism and authoritarianism.

The emergence of what has usually been called the 3M's[5] in Indian politics –mandal, mandir and market, was the defining feature of Indian politics from this period. These three issues which dominated the political agenda of the 1990s simultaneously brought together and sharply divided the political competitors in multiple ways.[6] In short, a political crisis of historic dimensions was unfolding before us with these developments which proved that the spirit of an age, as of a people is to be judged not by the finality of its achievements but by the sincerity of its endeavours.

Notes and References:

1   Sumit Ganguly, The Introduction to *The State of India's Democracy* (ed.) Sumit Ganguly, Larry Diamond and Marc F. Plattner, Baltimore, MD: Johns Hopkins University Press, 2007. pp.ix- xxvii.

2.   K .P. Karunakaran, 'The Encounter Between Hinduism and Modern Politics', *Onlooker*, November 15, 1990, p.6.

3.   Rajni Kothari, *State Against Democracy; In Search of Humane Governance*, Delhi, 1988, p.40.

4.   Dilip Simeon, 'Social Radicalism in Indian Politics', *The Illustrated Weekly of India*, December 1-2,1990.

5   Yogendra Yadav, 'Open Contest, Closed Options', *Seminar* (534),pp.62-69.

6   Yogendra Yadav ,'Politics', in Marshall m. Bouton and Philip Oldenburg (eds.), *India Briefing; A Transformative Fifty Years'*, London, M.E. Sharpe, pp.3-38.

Appendices

APPENDIX - I

Election Manifesto of Janata Party - 1977

To Generate Fearlessness and to Revive Democracy, the Janata Party's Political Charter Envisages:

1. Lift the Emergency.

2. Restore the fundamental freedoms that have been suspended by Presidential order;

3. Repeal MISA, release all political detainees, and review all other unjust laws;

4. Enact laws to ensure that no political or social organisation is banned without independent judicial enquiry;

5. Seek to rescind the 42nd Amendment;

6. Amend Article 352 of the Constitution to prevent its abuse in the interest of an individual or group;

7. Move to amend Article 356 to ensure that the power to impose President's Rule in the States is not misused to benefit the ruling party or any favoured faction within it;

8. Introduce electoral reforms after a careful consideration of suggestions made by various committees including the Tarkunde Committee and, in particular, consider proposals for recall of errant legislators and for reducing election costs, as well as for reducing voting age from, 21 to 18;

9.   Repeal the amendment to the Representation of the people Act which redefines corrupt practices and electoral offence by certain individuals beyond the scrutiny of the courts;

10.   Re-establish the Rule of Law;

11.   Restore the authority of the Judiciary and safeguard the independence and integrity of the Bar;

12.   Ensure that all individuals, including those who hold high office, are equal before law;

13.   Assure the right to peaceful and non-violent protest;

14.   Abolish censorship and end all harassment to newspapers, journals, publishers and printing presses.

15.   Safeguard the freedom of the Press by repealing the Prevention of Publication of Objectivable Matters Act, and restore the immunity that the Press previously enjoyed in reporting legislative proceedings.

16.   Ensure that All-India Radio, Doordarshan and the Films Division are converted into genuinely autonomous bodies that are politically objective and free from governmental interference:

17.   Ensure that news agencies are completely independent of the Government and are not given the right to monopoly;

18.   Delete property from the list of Fundamental Rights and instead, affirm the right to work;

19.   Ensure that Government employees are not victimised, are freed of political pressure, and are not compelled to execute illegal orders and unlawful actions. Their right to access to Courts will be restored.

The Janata Party's Economic Charter Envisages

1.   Deletion of property as a Fundamental Right;

2. Affirmation of the right to work and a full employment strategy;

3. Stress on Gandhian values of austerity, 'Antyodaya' and a decentralised economy.

4. An end to destitution within ten years;

5. Appropriate technology for self-reliance,

6. New planning priorities, notably the primacy of agriculture, agrarian reforms and more favourable terms of trade and higher allocations for the rural sector.

7. Narrowing down rural-urban disparities and a new rural urban nexus,

8. Emphasis on wage goods production for mass consumption.

9. Statutory reservation of spheres of production for small scale and cottage industries.

10. A wage ad price policy, raising the minimum tax exemption limit to Rs.10,000 and exemption of land revenue on all holdings below 2.5 hectares,

11. Redistributive taxation and excise in lieu of sales tax,

12. Formulation of a national water policy and a national energy policy.

13. Environmental care.

The Janata Party's Social Charter Envisages:

1. Education reform with middle schooling for all within 12 years;

2. Eradication of illiteracy;

3. Safe drinking water for all;

4. Stress on community and preventive health, and measures towards group health insurance;

5.   A new village movement.

6.   Low-cost building and mass public housing;

7.   A policy regarding urbanisation,

8.   A comprehensive scheme of social insurance,

9.   Family planning as part of a larger population policy package, without coercion.

10. A new deal for the scheduled castes and tribes with special machinery to guarantee their rights and interests.

11. A Civil Rights Commission,

12. Automatic machinery for combating corruption,

13. Women's rights and youth welfare.

14. Legal aid and inexpensive justice.

15. Fostering people's initiative and voluntary action.

APPENDIX - II

Percentage of Votes Obtained by Political parties and the party position in Lok Sabha (1952-1989)

Year	% of votes polled	No. of Seats	Cong/Cong (I) Seats	%	CPI Seats	%	KMPP/PSP & SSP Seats	%	BJS/BJP Seats	%	BLD/Janata Dal Seats	%	Janata (S) Seats	%	Lok Dal DMKP Seats	%	Others Seats	%	Independents Seats	%
1952	45.7	489	364	45.0	16	3.3			9	5.8	3	3.1					59	27.0	38	15.9
1957	47.7	494	371	47.0	27	8.9			19	10.4		5.9					31	7.6	42	19.4
1962	55.4	494	361	44.7	29	9.9			12	6.8	4	6.4					58	21.0	20	11.1
1967	61.3	520	233	40.8	23	5.0	19	4.4	36	8.0	14	9.4					89	18.8	35	13.7
1971	55.3	518	352	43.7	23	4.7	25	5.1	5	34	35	7.4					77	27.3	14	8.4
1977	60.3	542	154	34.5	7	2.8	22	4.3			22		295	41.3			55	11.5	9	5.5
1980	57.0	542a	353	42.7	11	2.6	36	6.1					31	19.0	41	9.4	48*	13.8	9	6.4
1984	64.1	542b	415	48.1	6	2.7	22	5.7					10	6.7	3	3	79*	15.7	5	8.1
1989		542c	193	40.3	12	2.7	33	6.5			141	18.3					59d	20.4	-	-

a)   Election were not held in 12 Constituencies in Assam and one in Meghalaya.

b)   Elections took place in Assam and Punjab only in 1985.

c)   Elections were not held in Assam: Elections were held in 525 constituencies

d)   This figure includes seats obtained by independents and other parties.

*   In 1980 Others include, Congress (U)-13, DMK-16, Anna DMK-2, IUML-3, National Conference-5 and Akali Dal-2,

      In 1984 others include-congress (S)-8, Telugu, Desam-28, AIADMK-12, DMK-1, Akali Dal-7AGP-7, RSP-3, Forward Bloc-2, National Conference-3, Kerala Congress (J)-2, Kerala Congress (M)-I, Congress (J)-1, Workers and Peasants Party-1.

*Source: For the Lok Sabha Lok Sabha Elections 1952 to1984, Reports of the Election Commission; for the 1989 Elections, preliminary analysis done by the UNI.

APPENDIX - III

Memorandum on Centre-State Relations

The following document on Centre-State Relations was adopted by the West Bengal Cabinet at its meeting held on December 1, 1977.

The question of Centre-State relations is crucial to the preservation of the unity and integrity of India within the frame work of its linguistic, cultural and other diversities. The several linguistic and cultural groups that inhabit the country were united before Independence in their common aspiration for freedom from colonial bondage. They are today united in their common aspiration to build a prosperous life for themselves as well as to develop full national resources free from imperialist interference and according to their respective socio-economic, linguistic and cultural needs. The struggle for realising these common aspirations makes it incumbent on the governments at the Centre and the States, the political parties and the people at large to recognise the need for unity in diversity.

1. The Constitution that emerged after Independence, though described as federal, was essentially unitary in character. It clothes the Centre with more powers at the expense of the autonomy of the States. That is why the "Concurrent" list has as many as 47 items. Since the adoption of the Constitution, the tendency had been to make greater inroads into the powers of States. This was facilitated by the fact that the same political party was in power at the centre and in all the states, except for short durations and, that too, in only a few States.

2. During the last two decades, while the demand has been growing for greater powers to the states so as to make States' autonomy real and effective, there have been persistent efforts to erode even the limited powers of the states and reduce the democratic functioning of the governments there. The right of the people to manage their affairs even within the limited sphere allotted in the states List of

the Constitution has been sought to ne reduced to a farse. For this purpose, all manner of pressures had been used, sometimes formally through the power of the Centre, sometimes indirectly by denying finances and other resource s, etc., to non-Congress Governments and by applying pressure on the Chief Ministers of the Congress Party through the organisation and leadership. During the last ten years, the Centre's tentacles have further spread to the states even in the sphere of law and order, which is formally a State subject, through the creation of the Central Reserve Police, the Border Security Force, the Industrial Security Force Etc. By the 42nd Amendment to the Constitution, Education, which was a State subject, was transferred to the Concurrent List. The process has now reached a stage when it threats to reduce the states to the status of subordinate departments of the Centre under the aegis of the Central Home Ministry. The Emergency immensely accelerated the process the actions taken in those twenty months sought to make it clear beyond doubt that the State Ministries and legislatures faced the perpetual threat of being removed by hook or crook, if they did not toe the line of the Centre.

3. The issue of Centre-State relations has assumed a new significance in the changed political context. Different parties are in office in the different States and in the Centre. This is a welcome departure from the one-party authoritarian rule of the Congress. It is a part of the democratic aspirations of the people that federal principle should be correctly understood and applied so that this multi-party democratic pattern may survive.

4. In a country like India, with such diversities in race, religion, language and culture, national integration can be achieved only through conscious voluntary efforts. Devolution of powers may help ward off fissiparous tendencies instead of encouraging them. A strong and unified India can be one in which the democratic aspirations and the distinctiveness of the people of the different States are respected and not treated with disdain. We are definitely for strong states, but on no account do we want a weak Centre. The concept of strong States is not necessarily in contradiction to that of a strong Centre. Once their respective spheres of authority are clearly marked out. The Preamble to the Constitution should

be amended to include the word 'federal' in the description of the Republic of India Consequential changes should also be made replacing the word 'Union' by the expression 'Federation' in all places.

5. To protect the States autonomy, an amendment to Article 248 should e made to the effect that the legislature of a state should have exclusive power to make any law with respect to any matter not enumerated in the Union or Concurrent List. as against the present provisions which reserves this right to Parliament. In other words, the residual powers of the federation should lie with the units and not with the centre.

The States have to act in such a way while exercising the full rights in their own sphere that they do not transgress the spheres allotted to the Central Government; the latter too, on its part, should not interfere in the sphere of the States, both legislative and executive.

Article 249 giving power to Parliament to legislate on a subject in the State List under the plea of national interest should be deleted.

6. While enlarging the scope of the States' sphere, we must also try to preserve and strengthen the Union authority by subjects that could be carried out by the Union authority and not by any single State, such as defence, foreign affairs including foreign trade, currency and communications and economic coordination. The role of the Centre should be one of coordination. In areas such as planning, fixing of prices, wages, etc; the Centre may not only coordinate but also issue general direction.

In the matter of planning and economic coordination, however, the centre will have to conform to the general guidelines laid down by the National Development Council, in which the States will have representation along with the centre. At the moment, neither the Council nor the planning Commission is specifically deferred to in the Constitution. This lacuna may be closed by introducing a separate Article, which should also state clearly that the composition of the Planning Commission will be determined by the National Development Council, Loans and grants for development purposes are now the prerogative of the Planning Commission. It is thus important that the states have some say in the manner of operation of the Commission. But nothing beyond foreign relations, defence, communications, currency and related matters should be the exclusive domain of the Centre. The latter should help the States develop in their own way, with more powers and resources at their command.

7. Industrial and power or irrigation schemes which concern more than one State have to be kept in the Union List so that there can be a common policy and final decision in regard to these multi-state projects will be enumerated by the Union Government while the execution and implementation should be done through the State Governments.

In matters concerning, industrial licensing, etc. major modifications in the allocation of powers between the Centre and the States are called for. The Lists in the Seventh Schedule should be reformulated so that States may be given exclusive powers in respect of certain categories of industries.

The right of the Central Reserve Police or other police forces the Union Government may raise to operate in the States is to be withdrawn. The subjects of law and order and the police should be fully in the State sphere, and the Centre should not interfere with its own specially created forces.

8. The Articles regarding the Finance Commission and the distribution of revenues should be amended to provide for 75 per cent of the total revenues raised by the Centre from all sources for allocation to different States by the Finance Commission. This is necessary to end the mendicant status of the states.

In what proportion and on what principles this 75 per cent of the total realisation shall be divided between the States shall be decided by the Finance Commission.

It should not be the job of the Finance Commission to decide on the proportion or revenues to be distributed between the Centre and the sates. It task should be only to fix the proportion each State should get from the total financial realisation by the centre, 75 per cent of which is to be allotted to the states.

Article 280, clause 2, sub-clause (a), which provides "the distribution between the Union and the States of net proceeds of the taxes which are to be or may be divided between the Union and the States", should be omitted and the entire clause be redrafted so as to make it clear that it is the duty of the Commission to make recommendations to the President as to the allocation between the States of their respective shares of the proceeds.

The states must also be accorded more powers for imposing taxes on their own, and to determine the limits of public borrowing in their respective cases. The right of the Union Government to tax property and income to the States in certain cases as provided in Article 280 clause 2 and 3 should be removed. Further, the right of the Union Ministry to put restrictions on trade and commerce and intervene within a State as provided in Article 302 should be deleted. To achieve these objectives, the Seventh Schedule enumerating Union, State and Concurrent Lists should be suitably amended.

9. Articles 356 and 357 which enable the President to dissolve a State Government or its Assembly or both should be deleted. In the case of a Constitutional breakdown in a State, Provision must be made for the democratic step of holding election and installing a new Government as in the case of the Centre. Similarly, Article 360, which empowers the President to interfere in a State administration on the grounds of a threat to financial instability or credit of India should be deleted.

10. In order to enforce the principle of equality of the federating units and to protect further erosion of States' autonomy, it is suggested that elections to the Rajya Sabha also should be directly by the people at the same time as the Lok Sabha elections, all States must have equal representation in the Rajya Sabha except those with a population of less than three million. Both houses must have equal powers.

11. All-India services like the IAS, the IPS etc; whose officers are posted to the States but remain under the supervision and disciplinary control of the Central Government, must be abolished. There should be only Union Services and States Services and recruitment to them should be made respectively by the Union Government and State Government concerned. Personnel of the Union Services should be under the disciplinary control of the Union Government and those of the State Services under the disciplinary control of the respective State Governments. the Central Government should have no jurisdiction over the personnel of the State Services.

12. Article 368 should be so amended as to ensure that no amendment of the Constitution is possible without the concurrence of two thirds of the members present and voting in each House of Parliament.

13. Article 3 of the Constitution which gives powers to the Parliament to change the area of a State unilaterally, should be suitably amended so as to ensure that the name and area of a state cannot be changed by the Parliament without specific consent for that by the State Legislature concerned. In the cise of a conflict between two or more States in respect of territory steps would be taken to settle the conflict in accordance with the provisions already made in the Constitution, for settlement of other conflicts (e.g. use of water resources of the same river flowing through a number of States) between the States.

14. Languages mentioned in the English Schedule should be allowed in the work of the Governments at the Centre and in the States at all levels. Any citizen of India will have the right to use his mother-tongue in his dealings with any branch of the Government u to the highest stage. English should continue to be used for all the official purposes of the Union along with Hindu till as long as the people of the non-Hindi regions so desire. It may be necessary to further amend the Eighth Schedule to include certain other languages, such as Nepali.

15. The special status of Kashmir within the Indian Union, as laid down in Article 370 of the Constitution, should be retained. The

way this Article had been worked by the Congress Government at the Centre had raised grave doubts and suspicion among the people of the State. These must be removed now, particularly in view of the fact that the leaders of the State Government have underlined the Instrument of Accession to India.

APPENDIX - IV

Electoral Commitments of Janata Dal/National Front

1. Right to work as a fundamental right that is justifiable. The Constitution will be amended towards this end.

2. Uniform and universal education to all children, including girls through neighbourhood schools upto the high school level. Steps to vocationalise education, upgrade the status of teachers and improve their conditions of work and salaries.

3. A new deal for farmers and for rural India through (a) channelling 50 per cent of the plan investment for agriculture and related works; (b) writing off the debts of agricultural workers rural artisans and small farmers; (c) crop insurance; (d) parity in the prices of agricultural and industrial produce; (e) removal of all restrictions on movement of agricultural produce and its value added products.

4. A national minimum wage for workers in all sectors including the unorganised sector.

5. Rehabilitation of workers in sick industries and effective worker participation in management.

6. Action on the accommodations of the Mandal Commission to better the lot of other backward classes.

7. Property rights for women and 30 percent job reservation in public employment, Panchayati Raj and local bodies speedy and stringent punishment for all offences against women.

8. Conversion of the State-owned electronic media into autonomous corporations.

9. Immediate legal and diplomatic steps to identify and bring back to the country Indian money stacked away in foreign banks followed by prosecution of the offenders.

10. Banning of foreign capital and multinationals from low priority and consumer goods sectors and emphasis on Swadeshi and self-reliance.

11.   Effective and genuine decentralisation of economic and political power.

12.   Assurance of fulfilment of essential needs of clean drinking water, food, clothing, shelter and health to all.

13.   Amendment of Article 311 in order to restore to the Government employees safeguards against arbitrary dismissal.

14. Assurance to minorities against interference in their personal laws and religious, cultural and educational institutions; special arrangements to promote employment and education among them. Setting up of a special composite force of members of all communities to deal with communal and caste riots. Ensure due status to Urdu on the basis of the Gujral Committee report.

15. The backlog in reservation for Schedules Castes and Tribes shall be filled expeditiously by taking special measures. The policy of reservations in the political field, employment and education shall continue. The SC/ST Commission, Minorities Commission and Commission on the status of women shall be give statutory powers.

16. Thorough-going tenancy reforms, establishment of special courts, cancellation of fraudulent transactions and end to evictions.

APPENDIX – V

Text of the letter to the Bharatiya Janata Party from the National Front

Dear Shri Advaniji,

We are sure that you agree with us that the people of India have given a clear and unmistakable verdict against the Congress (I) misrule and for a change of Government at the Centre. The seat adjustments among the various Opposition parties have greatly helped us in defeating the Congress (I). It is now the sacred duty of all of us to see that this mandate of the people is not frustrated and the formation of a non-Congress (I) Government is not delayed to give effect to the hopes and aspirations of the people.

The National Front has, therefore, decided to shoulder this onerous responsibility of approaching the President and stake its claim to form the new government.

May we seek the support of your party in this effort.

With kind regards.

Yours sincerely,

(Sd/-) N.T.Rama Rao, (Chairman)

(Sd/-) Vishwanath Pratap Singh, (Convenor)

Shri.L.K.Advani,

President, Bharatiya Janata Party.

APPENDIX-VI

The text of the reply from Mr. L.K. Advani President, BJP to National Front.

Dear Shri Rama Rao Ji and Shri.V.P. Singh Ji,

I am in receipt of your letter dated 28th November, 1989 seeking the BJP's support in forming a National Front Government.

I agree that the people have given a clear verdict against the Rajiv Government. But simultaneously this is also true that there has been no positive verdict in favour of any one party, or in favour of the five-party National Front.

Your letter amounts to seeking unconditional support from the BJP for a minority Government. The BJP has some reservations extending such support to your Government. Our two principal reservations are:

i. The National Front and BJP fought these elections on two separate manifestoes, not on a common manifesto. A manifesto is a party's solemn commitment to the people. Our two manifestoes have several common features, such as grant of autonomy to Akashwani and Doordarshan, enactment of a Right to Information Act. incorporating Right to work as a fundamental right in the Constitution, elimination of corruption by the creation of an institutional watch dog like the Lokpal, taking steps to give debt relief and ensure remunerative prices to the farmer etc. But there are aspects on which the two manifestoes differ. We would like the N.F. government to confine its governmental programme to issues on which we agree.

ii. The main constituent of the National Front is the Janata Dal, Ever since its launching, J.D. leadership, by its utterances and actions has been consciously trying to convey to the people an impression that it regards the BJP as a communal party, and that it would rather sit in the opposition than ever share power with it. The J.D's public postures have thwarted the building up of any abiding relationship of trust and friendship between our parties. If it is acknowledged by the JD that though the J A and BJP differ on issues like Art 370, Uniform Civil Code, Human Rights Commission, Ram Janam Bhoomi, etc., the J.D does not regard the BJP as communal, that would go a long way in removing misgivings in our rank and file.

I hope the N F will take note of these reservations and exert to obviate them.

The BJP is keen to see that the Ninth General Election marks the end of Congress rule in New Delhi. It is, therefore, that even while expressing these reservations, we have not made our support to you conditional to your agreeing to remove them. In response to your letter, the BJP wishes to convey to you its readiness to give general but critical support of the N F Government.

With kind regards.

Yours Sincerely

(Sd/-) L.K. Advani.

N.T. Rama Rao, Chairman, and V.P.Singh, (Convener) of The National Front, 16, Windsor Place, New Delhi.

Bibliography

Documents:

Reports of the Election Commission 1952-84, New Delhi, 1985.

The Election Archives , New Delhi, 1989.

Articles:

Aiyar, A.P.'Two years of Janata', *The Illustrated Weekly of India*, 18-24 Mach, 1979.

Ahmd, Bashiruddhin. 'The Crisis of Change', *Seminar*, No. 242, October, 1979.

Almond, G.A. 'The Return of the State', *American Political Science Review*, 82:3 September, 1988.

Babu, Ramesh , 'Opportunity for the Opposition', *Seminar*, No.368, April 1990.

Banerjee, Sumanta, 'Revolutionary Movements in a Post-Marxian Era', Economic and Political Weekly, Vol.XLVII (18), May 5, 2012, p.57.

Chandan, Amarjit. 'North After the Rout', *Economic and Political Weekly*, 19 January 1980.

Chandrasekhar, S. 'Betrayal of Janata Party', *The Indian Express*, 16 August 1979.

Chittaranjan, C.R. 'Will the Communists of India Unite?' *The Illustrated weekly of India*, 7-13 January 1979.

Dandavate, Madhu. 'Crisis Rooted in Summit Power Politics', *The Indian Express,* 11 August 1979.

Ganguly, Tarun. 'The CPI (M)'s Real Politick', *Sunday*, 4 November 1979.

Goyal, D.R. 'Confrontation with Democracy', *Seminar*, No. 127, March 1970.

Gupta, Babani Sen. 'Communist Power', *Seminar*, No.248, April 1980.

Gupta, Babani Sen. 'Limits of Consensus Politics', *Economic and Political Weekly*, April, 7, 1990.

Karunakaran, K.P. 'The Encounter Between Hinduism and Modern Politics', *Onlooker*, November 15, 1990. [31]

Kailash, K. K. 'Competition and Coalition Formation in the New Party System', in E. Sridharan (ed.), Coalition Politics in India: Selected Issues at the Centre and the States, New Delhi, Academic Foundation, 2014.

Katyal, K.K. 'Craving for a Change', *The Hindu*, 4 December 1979.

Katyal, K.K. 'Towards Communist Reconciliation?' *The Hindu*, 10 April 1978.

Kothari, Rajni. 'Delivering Goods', *Seminar*, No. 242, October 1979.

Kothari, Rajani. 'Grassroot Movements: The Search for Alternatives', *The Illustrated Weekly of India*, April 29, 1984.

Limaye, Madhu. 'The State of Opposition', *The Hindu*, 2 December, 1988.

Mitra, Sumit. 'The Past Catches Up', *India Today*, 16-31 March, 1979.

Omvedt, Gail, 'The Anti-Caste Movement and Discourse of Power', in Niraja gopal Jayal (ed.), *Democracy in India*, New Delhi, Oxford University Press,2001.

Pachuri, Pankaj. 'Election Gamble', *India Today*, November 15, 1990.

Parthasarathy, Malini. 'The Winning Strategy', *Frontline*, December 9-22, 1990.

Punekar, S.D. & Brahmprakash. 'Promises and Performance', *The Illustrated Weekly of India*, 18-24 March, 1978.

Rao, K. Raghavendra, 'Understanding the Indian State: A Historical- Materialist Exercise', in Zoya Hasan, et al., The State , Political Process,and Identity: Reflections on Modern India, New Delhi, Sage Publications,1989.

Ram, Mohan. 'The Compromise Game', *Seminar*, No. 362, October, 1989.

Ram, Mohan. 'Janatha Portents', *Economic and political Weekly*, 29 January, 1977.

Ram, Mohan. 'The Key Issue', *Economic and Political Weekly*, Annual number, 1977.

Rodrigues, Valerian, 'The Communist Parties in India', in Peter Ronald deSouza (eds.) *India's Political Parties*, New Delhi, Sage Publications, 2006.

Roy, Ranjit. 'The CPI Left Alienated', *Sunday*, 4 November, 1979.

Shivlal. 'Party Politics in India: Janata's Fiasco of Promises and Performance', *The Election Archives,* New Delhi, 1979.

Simeon, Dilip. 'Social Radicalism in Indian Politics', *The illustrated Weekly of India*. (Weekened) December 1-2, 1990.

Tabib, Rasheed. 'Should the Congress be one?' , *The Illustrated Weekly of India*, 2-8 April, 1978.

Tellis, Olga. 'Janta Deserves Better Image', *Sunday*, 30 December, 1979.

Urs, Devaraj. 'Pragmatism is the only Answer to India's Problems', *The Indian Express,* 17 August, 1979.

Varma, Kewal. 'Is a Red Sun Rising?', *Sunday*, 4 November, 1979.

Vora, Pankaj, 'The BJP Game Plan', *The Hindu Weekly Edition*, November 11, 1990.

Yadav, Yogendra, 'Open Contest, Closed Options', *Seminar* (534).

Yadav, Yogendra ,'Politics',in Marshall M. Bouton and Philip Oldenburg (eds.), *India Briefing; A Transformative Fifty Years'*, London,M.E. Sharpe.

Zarkaria, Rafiq. 'The Congress', *The Illustrated Weekly of India*, 29 January-4 February, 1979.

Books:

Abbas, K.A. *20th March 1977; A Day Like any Other Day*, New Delhi, 1978.

Balaram, N.E. *A Short History of the Communist Party f India*, Trivandrum, 1967.

Basu, D.D. *Introduction to the Constitution of India*, Calcutta, 1990.

Carr, Robert., Marver Bernstein and Walter Murphy, *American Democracy in Theory and Practice*, Newyork, 1975.

Carter, April. *Authority and Democracy*, London, 1979.

Dowse, Robert E. & John A. Hughes, *Political Sociology*, London, 1972.

Ganguly, Sumit, Larry Diamond and Marc F.Plattner, *The State of India's Democracy*, Baltimore, MD: Johns Hopkins University Press, 2007.

Ganguly, Sumit and Rahul Mukherji, *India Since 1980*, New Delhi, Cambridge University Press,2011.

Gupta, D.C. *Indian Government and Politics*, New Delhi, 1988.

Gramsci, Antonio, *Selections from Prison Note Books,* Ne Hoare,O & Nowell, G.S. (ed.), London, 1971.

Johari, J.C. *Indian Government and Politics*, Delhi, 1989.

Jones, Morris W. H. *The Government and Politics of India*, New Delhi, 1971.

Kothari, Rajani. *State Against Democracy: In Search of Human Governance,* Delhi, 1988.

Maravall, Jose. *Dictatorship and Political Dissent,* London, 1978.

Mirchandani, G.G. *32 Million Judges*, New Delhi, 1977.

Naik, J.A. *From Total Revolution to Total Failure*, New Delhi, 1979.

Narasimhan, V.K. *Democracy Redeemed,* New Delhi, 1977.

Nayarm Kuldip. *The Judgement,* New Delhi, 1977.

Nossiter,T.J. *Marxist State Governments in India: Politics, Economics and Society,* London, 1988.

Palmer, Norman, D. *Elections and Political Development: The South Asian Experiment,* New Delhi, 1975.

Saihgal, Nayantara. *Indira Gandhi's Emergence and Style,* New Delhi, 1978.

Selborne, David. *Through the Indian Looking Glass,* Bombay, 1982.

Shakar, S.L. (ed.). *The Sixth General Election to Lok Sabha,* New Delhi, 1977.

Sinha, Sachidanad. *Emergency in Perspective: Reprieve and Challenge,* New Delhi, 1977.

Siwach, J.R. *Dynamics of Indian Government and Politics,* New Delhi, 1990.

Thakur, Janardan. *All the Janata Men,* New Delhi, 1978.

Times of India Directory and Year Book , New Delhi, 1990

Tiwari,V.N. *12 Willington Crescent: Indian Politics at the Cross Roads*, Delhi, 1979.

Wolpert, Stanley. *A New History of India*, New York, 1977.

News Papers & Periodicals:

The Hindu (Coimbatore & Madras)

The Hindustan Times (New Delhi)

The Indian Express (Cochin)

The Statesman (New Delhi)

The Times of India (Bombay)

Economic and Political Weekly (Bombay)

Frontline (Madras)

India Today (New Delhi)

Kerala Saddam (Quilon)

Link Indias News Magazine (New Delhi)

Onlooker (Bombay)

Seminar (New Delhi)

Sunday (Calcutta)

The Illustrated weekly of India (Bombay)

Index

9789389620177